Navigating Change

How to Go From Trauma to Transformation

Patricia Ariadne, Ph.D.

Author of Bridging Night and Day: Decoding the Hidden Messages of Your Dreams

Copyright © 2016 by by Patricia Ariadne, Ph.D.
All rights reserved.
ISBN: 978-0-9974680-1-4
Printed in the USA

No part of this publication may be reproduced or transmitted in any form or by any means, electronic or mechanical, including photocopying, recording, or by any information storage and retrieval system, without written permission of the publisher except in the case of brief quotations in articles or reviews.

Sothis Press
Encinitas, CA

SothisPress.com

Table of Contents

Introduction vii
- The Essence of Life is Change viii
- Voluntary and Involuntary Change viii
- Change and Transition ix
- Resilience ix
- Removing Blocks ix
- Tools for Change x
- The Dark Knight of the Soul x
- Personal and Cultural Change xi
- About the Author xi

Chapter 1: Why We Need Change 1
- Why Is Change Necessary? 2
  - Journaling: Three Turning Points 3
- Change and Transition Are Not the Same 4
  - Journaling: Major Change & Your Emotions 4
  - Exercise: Ritual: Forgiving the Past 6
- Stages of a Transition 7
  - Stage One: Stage of Endings or Loss 7
  - Stage Two: Middle or Neutral Stage 8
    - Journaling: Your Middle Zone 10
  - Stage Three: Stage of Beginnings or Renewal 12
    - Exercise: Thinking From the End 13
- In The Next Chapter 13

Chapter 2: Resilience: What It Is, Who Has It, What It Looks Like 15
- What Is Resilience? 16
- Who Is Resilient? 16
  - Quiz: How Much Do You Know About Resilience? 18
- Qualities of Resilient People 21
  - Journaling: Your Qualities of Resilience 23
  - Journaling: Qualities to Strengthen 24
  - Check List: Rate Your Resilience Quotient 25
- Persistence and Flexibility 26

- In The Next Chapter ... 27

Chapter 3: Removing Blocks To Resilience ... 29
- Block #1: Excessive Stress ... 30
  - De-Stress: Set Your Burdens Down... ... 30
  - Stress Busters ... 31
  - Humor Helps! ... 32
    - Journaling: Reducing Your Stress ... 33
- Block #2: Overwhelming Fears ... 34
  - Journaling: Dealing with Fear ... 34
  - Learning to Take Risks ... 37
    - Journaling: Six Areas of Life ... 37
- Block #3: Placating Behavior ... 41
  - Saying Adios to the Pleaser ... 41
  - Our "Other Side" ... 41
    - Journaling: Getting in Touch With the "Pleaser Self" ... 42
    - Exercise #1: Transforming the "Pleaser Self" ... 43
    - Exercise #2: Standing Your Ground ... 44
- In The Next Chapter ... 44

Chapter 4: Building Resilience: Tools For Change ... 45
- Tool #1: Tune Into Your Dreams ... 46
  - Dreams Light the Way ... 46
  - Dreams Bring Clarity ... 46
    - Exercise: Dream a Little Dream ... 48
- Tool #2: Try Journaling ... 48
  - Partnering with Life ... 48
  - Benefits of Journaling ... 49
  - A Gratitude Journal ... 51
    - Quiz: Take an Online Gratitude Quiz ... 52
- Tool #3: Boost Your Resilience Via Media Tools ... 52
  - Activity: Choose One! ... 53
- Tool #4: Balance Your Masculine and Feminine Qualities ... 54
  - The Masculine-Feminine Continuum ... 54
  - A Matter of Opposites ... 54
  - Extreme Qualities Become Shadow Qualities ... 55
  - Balance Brings Health and Wholeness ... 56
    - Journaling: Where on the Continuum? ... 56

- Inventory: The BEM Sex Role Inventory — 58
- In The Next Chapter — 58

Chapter 5: The Dark Night Of Soul — 61
- Post-Traumatic Growth: Bouncing Forward — 62
- Golden Nuggets of Meaning — 62
- The Dark Night of Soul — 63
  - Strange Symptoms — 64
  - Triggering Events — 65
  - What Can You Do? — 66
  - Who Gets Through the Dark Night of Soul? — 67
  - What is the Purpose of the Dark Night? — 68
  - What Are the Benefits? — 68
  - More Information on the Dark Night of the Soul — 69
- Quiz: Take a Post-Traumatic Growth Questionnaire! — 69
- Journaling: Character Strengths — 70
- In The Next Chapter — 71

Chapter 6: Individual Transformation And Societal Change — 73
- Take Charge of Change — 74
- Responding to Trends: Stephen's Story — 74
  - Journaling: What Changes Do You Foresee? — 75
- Possible Trends of the Future — 77
  - Demographic Change — 77
  - Fourth-Wave Feminism — 78
  - Happiness and Authenticity — 78
  - Spirituality — 78
  - Climate Change — 79
  - Robotics — 79
  - Medicine — 80
  - The Work Force — 80
  - Black Swan Events — 81
- New Expressions of Life Experience — 81
  - Chart: Conditions of the Past in Transition — 81
  - Strategic Social Change — 82
- An Interactive Relationship — 83
- Shadow Work — 84
- Map of Change — 84

• Exercise: Mapping Your Steps to Change	85
• The Final Step	86

Acknowledgments 87

Footnotes 88

Bibliography 89

Appendices 91
- Life Events Stress Scale — 92
- Dark Night of Soul Self-Test Inventory — 94
- The Four R's for Reducing Stress — 97
- Dr. Ariadne's Books — 98

INTRODUCTION

Change is the only constant.

~Bashar

All that you touch
You Change.
All that you Change
Changes you.
The only lasting truth
is Change.
God
is Change.

~Octavia E. Butler

The Essence of Life is Change

Most people fear change. When they see others facing tumultuous life change, they often shake their heads and mumble, "That's too bad" or "Bad break." People sometimes think that others are faced with troubling events because of poor decision-making or simply bad luck. In my psychotherapy practice, I often see people who, prior to seeing me, made great efforts to avoid change in their lives. When they could no longer dodge the chaos of change, they knocked on my office door. The irony is that change is actually built into the human life design: there is no other way to grow in life *except* through change!

Voluntary and Involuntary Change

Both types of change--*voluntary* and *involuntary*—demand adjustment (you adapt to the situation) or modification (you change the situation/environment to suit yourself). Voluntary changes are ones you choose to make and prepare for, such as quitting a job, beginning a family, taking early retirement, or starting your own business. In this type of change, you most often modify a situation in your life to more closely align with your long-range goals. When you make a satisfying voluntary change, you often feel that you are the "captain of your own ship" and life is at your command.

Involuntary changes, on the other hand, are changes that blindside you and appear beyond your control. These can include a sudden change in health, a death in the family, an unexpected divorce, or an abrupt lay-off from work. Most people initially react to involuntary changes with fear, anger, and depression. These types of changes force you to adapt yourself, sometimes very quickly, to a new situation. Involuntary changes are usually difficult to manage and may have a domino effect on other areas of your life: for instance, an unanticipated job loss may result in the eventual foreclosure of your house or in bankruptcy proceedings. However, such unforeseen changes can also be gateways to new opportunities, which can eventually bring about more fulfillment and a greater sense of purpose. An example might be that, after the initial panic due to losing your job, you acknowledge that you felt increasingly frustrated by your previous work in outside sales, and you now have the opportunity to work toward your life-long dream of opening a dog training academy. How you view your situation—and the tools you employ to deal with it—make the difference between feeling powerless and folding under pressure, or gaining the confidence to forge a new pathway in life.

> We choose voluntary changes and then prepare to make them; in contrast, involuntary changes blindside us, and we often react to these unexpected situations with fear and anxiety. Learning tools to deal with sudden change can help people both navigate through and learn from change.

Change and Transition

Change is an occurrence or event: a wedding; a death; a birth; a move to a new location; the start of a new job. *Transition*, on the other hand, is the period that follows a change. This is the time when you adapt to the change: you learn to give and take in a marital partnership, you mourn the loss of someone you love and learn how to move forward in life, you adjust to a new home by meeting your neighbors and discovering where the local schools, Trader Joe's, and Peet's Coffee & Tea are located. Transition can be seen as a three-part cycle, with a *Beginning*, a *Middle* or *Neutral Zone*, and an *Ending*. Each part has a particular significance and can be approached in ways that allow you to extract every possible benefit from each stage. The cycle of transition is discussed below in detail, using real-life examples and stories.

> **Change is the event that occurs in your life: a birth, a death, a wedding, a move. The transition is the period of time you need to adjust and adapt to the change.**

Resilience

Resilience is the ability to effectively deal with the challenge of change and transition. Resilience has been variously known as *bouncing back, overcoming adversity, staying the course, snapping back,* and *keeping the faith.* The first two chapters of this book will further define resilience and will explore the special qualities of resilient people. These chapters will look at the special importance of the qualities of persistence and flexibility as well as how greater resilience can be cultivated. Resilience involves not only *doubling down* and *powering through:* sometimes it requires patient waiting or "letting go and letting God." This is especially true in the middle stage of a transition, which will be described, along with the beginning and end stages, in **Chapter One**. Finally, there is the possibility of not only bouncing back from crisis but bouncing *forward*, or gaining from your difficulty, which will be more clearly examined in **Chapter Five**.

Removing Blocks

Even when life is going comparatively well, we often run into self-created stumbling blocks that prevent resilience in the face of life's challenges. This lack of persistent flexibility directly affects our ability to achieve our goals in life. The emotional and psychological blocks examined in this book include approaching life with excessive levels of stress, declining to take risks because of inhibiting fears, and looking outward to others in an attempt to please or placate them instead of first checking within ourselves to gauge what we really want. To deal with these blocks to resiliency, practical suggestions--such as journaling, learning risk-taking behaviors, and transforming the "pleaser self"-- are offered in **Chapter Three**.

Tools for Change

Change can be seen on a continuum of difficulty from a promotion at work with an increased workload, to the death of a family member or the contraction of a serious illness. This book will address all types of change but will particularly reflect on the kind that creates chaos and disorder in our lives; the sort that can transform and renovate us. Such change is seen as an opportunity to learn how to meet challenges--and life events in general--with greater strength and flexibility. We will learn how to experience change so that, instead of feeling the *rug has been pulled out from under us*, we discover that we can *dance on a moving rug!* We will examine how we can collaborate with life's crises so that we not only survive but experience *post-traumatic growth*, or invaluable personal and spiritual progress. Seen in this light, the outer and inner change that trauma creates is regarded as a way to become more aware of yourself, to better connect to your spiritual center, and ultimately, to nurture a desire to give back to others. In **Chapter Four**, I offer practical tools for change, among them dream work, active imagery, questions for reflective thought, and various activities and exercises, all to help you deal with immediate change and the transitions that follow.

> Tools for change include dream work. Your dreams can give you important information, especially when you are in the middle stage of transition where everything seems uncertain and confusing. Another useful approach is to train yourself to take greater risks in life, so that you are less controlled by fear in the face of change.

The Dark Night of Soul

When the change in an individual's life is a traumatic one--a divorce, the death of a loved one, or the loss of a home or job—the transition period may become extended as a difficult period of emotional and psychological upheaval. During this time, everything in the person's life is turned upside down, and the individual may experience

> Sometimes a transition develops into a long period of deep emotional and psychological upheaval. However, if this time is used for life-assessment and self-reflection, your personal crisis can lead to deep-seated transformation that ultimately brings greater psychological integration and well-being.

confusion, grief, anxiety, and depression. Sometimes this is called the *Dark Night of Soul*. What initially appears to be a negative experience, however, can prove to be a life-altering period of self-reflection and life-assessment, the healing of old wounds, greater personality integration, and the reprioritization of what's most important in life. In other words, an experience of post-traumatic stress can lead to post-traumatic growth. If navigated successfully, a dark night ordeal can lead the individual to a greater awareness of him or herself as a spiritual being. **Chapter Five** of this book will address this process, describing what a dark night looks like, what it means, ways to collaborate with it, and how to tell when you have successfully passed through it.

Personal & Cultural Change

When we learn how to more effectively handle change and transition in our own lives, the effects are far-reaching. We are influencing those around us in a positive way. Deep-seated change, such as that experienced during the dark night, entails taking a hard look at ourselves, peering into our darkest corners, and bringing to the surface the unconscious things we say and do. When we begin to take responsibility for ourselves, the result is that society itself is improved and uplifted. We mirror the society we live in, and since society is made up of people, it reflects back the changes that are occurring within the individuals who are living in it. Likewise, as major national and world events occur, such as severe weather patterns, economic downturns and various wars, we are affected by how these factors impact our lives. There is a reciprocal, shared experience between society and its citizens. In **Chapter Six**, we will briefly visit this interactive, interdependent relationship between personal change and cultural change.

About the Author

I speak to organizations and groups and write books and articles about change and transition because I have experienced so many changes in my own life! My childhood involved numerous moves, several schools, and many unsettling family changes and conflicts, resulting in my running away from home as a teen. Early adulthood included a young marriage, divorce, and a life-changing psychological and spiritual experience at thirty-two. Since then, I've experienced many ups 'n' downs, in the common areas of struggle--finances, jobs, housing, relationships--that most of us face in life. I have also spent a great deal of time coming to terms with early childhood trauma and family dysfunction. It isn't a surprise that I became focused on ways people can successfully change and adapt to new cycles of life experience!

I am currently a licensed psychotherapist whose primary interest is working with everyday people undergoing crisis in their lives; in fact, I call myself the *Transition Therapist.* I am dedicated to helping people utilize this difficult time as a springboard to greater psychological and spiritual growth. I have written several books, among them *Drinking the Dragon: Stories of the Dark Night of Soul,* along with a companion process workbook. For this book, I interviewed persons who describe particularly difficult periods of transition, which ultimately became positive journeys of transformation. In *Navigating Change,* I approach change and transition as challenges to grow by: it's a 180 degree mental turnabout to see difficulties as a means to becoming stronger and more fully alive and not merely as punishments unjustly visited upon us by fate or an angry god.

Aside from engaging in traditional one-on-one talk therapy, I also use several less conventional tools in my private practice, such as dream work. I find that this tool is invaluable during transition periods: dreams can point toward a new life purpose when we feel lost, confused, and uncertain. The first book in my *Transition Series, Bridging Night and Day: Decoding the Hidden Messages of Dreams,* addresses how dreams can serve as a *dipstick, plumb line,* or *read-out* to let us know where we are in our lives, especially when we are at the end of one cycle but not yet in a new one.

There are several more techniques I use to help people cope with and learn from the difficult, painful and confusing times in their lives. I practice active imagination or visualization work that involves resolving an emotional crisis and finding inspiration for the next step in life. Some of these methods involve specific ways to "cut ties," or let go of life patterns that have held individuals back from reaching their goals.

I have written this book to help the increasing numbers of people who are facing seriously difficult life challenges. As weather conditions, economic fluctuations, job market instability, and world and societal unrest and violence become more prevalent and volatile, people need to learn better coping strategies. In addition to suggesting life management skills, I want to explore the underlying significance of change and transition and how it is possible for persons to grow and transform through their troubles. I have organized *Navigating Change* with journal questions, quizzes and exercises to engage you. Let your journey begin!

CHAPTER ONE:
Why We Need Change

If we don't change, we don't grow. If we don't grow, we aren't really living.

~Gail Sheehy

Change is hardest at the beginning, messiest in the middle and best at the end.

~Robin S. Sharma

Why is Change Necessary?

What does change mean to you? For many people, change represents chaos and confusion. They fear losing control and perhaps, even losing what they have acquired in life. But progress does not always mean gain: we need to leave behind what we've outgrown to make room for something new to enter our lives. The story below illustrates this understanding:

> Retirement threw Sandra *for a loop*: she did not feel ready to retire. She found herself nursing a low-grade depression and experiencing bouts of anxiety. Unable to organize her time, she stayed in bed during the day, not bothering to get dressed. After working as a busy executive for several decades, she found her current life oppressive and meaningless. Sandra decided to enter psychotherapy to examine her options, figure out a *second act*, and to find a new lease on life. She had a deep yearning to be creatively expressive and to be of service. But first, she needed to mourn the passing of her former self—to let go of her previous job and the role she had identified with for so many years. She needed to assess her past in order to design her future. Sandra was being challenged to adjust to a new life cycle. Life was calling her to the task of change.

If you reflect on a period of difficult change and transition in your life, you can probably come up with a few things that you learned: you are stronger than you thought you were, you have a network of people you can depend on when *the chips are down*, you are able to forgive someone you feel has wronged you. Importantly, you learned that you could *survive!* And perhaps, beyond survival, you personally grew from the experience, becoming a better listener, more compassionate, and more patient with others.

Change is part of the natural rhythm of life, the process of death and renewal. Everything in nature is in the process of transforming, of building up or breaking down: molting, shedding, budding, wilting, gestating, rotting, cracking, rusting or propagating. Humans, too, have life cycles and developmental stages. You do not have to die in your physical life to experience death: it's felt when a friendship ends, when a pet dies, when there is a divorce, the end of a job, or retirement. But where there is an ending, there is also a beginning: you find a new friend, you buy another pet, you begin an intimate relationship, you get an exciting job offer, or you find a new creative outlet.

> **Change is a natural part of life. We constantly experience in everyday life what Elizabeth Kubler-Ross called *mini-deaths*. These mini-deaths include the end of friendships and romances, relocations to new areas to live, or an empty nest at home.**

Change is built into the human life design to help us learn new ways of thinking and of doing things. Change helps us to develop strength and understanding by dealing with obstacles. Ultimately, meeting new challenges makes us less complacent, so that we begin asking questions about life's deeper meaning. This book will provide you with tools to help you understand how to meet change and how to better navigate the transition period that follows it. Some of these tools require that we accommodate or adjust ourselves to the environment; others allow us to modify outer circumstances to suit us.

 *Journaling: Three Turning Points*

Quickly jot down three of the biggest turning points in your life. Chances are that at least one of these turning points involved a life crisis of some sort. What are one or two important things that you learned from having experienced this life crisis? How did you grow from having faced such a difficult time?

_____
_____
_____
_____
_____
_____
_____
_____
_____
_____
_____
_____
_____

Change & Transition Are Not the Same

Change is an event or occurrence: giving birth, starting a new job, retiring, contracting an illness. *Transition* follows the event and is usually a long period that involves both internal adaptations and outer modifications to a change. During the transition period, you can choose to change yourself (*adapt*) to deal with the event, such as reading books on baby care and development or taking a training course to better perform in a new job role. You can also change circumstances surrounding the event (*modify*) to better suit you, such as making arrangements when you are ill to work fewer hours or to quit a demanding job altogether to allow more time for healing.

> Change is a life event; transition is the period that follows and allows you to adapt to the change. During the transition period, it is important to reflect on what you have gained from the previous cycle and to process persistent negative emotions that need clearing.

Emotional adjustments are a part of the transition period, such as dealing with grief and loss when someone close to you dies, processing anger, betrayal, and other raw emotions during and after a divorce, or handling apprehension and anxiety when you begin a new job. When these emotions are left unresolved, they can negatively affect future behavior and interactions. Unfortunately, many people choose to escape the challenge of facing and healing these emotions by ramping up social activities, using electronics to distract themselves, self-medicating with prescription or recreational drugs, or making radical decisions--such as quitting a job or having an affair--that are only temporary diversions. This is the time to find a professionally trained ally--a licensed psychotherapist or clergy member, for example--in order to directly face and process these turbulent emotions. It's also important to examine the life event for the take-aways: what can you learn from the change and the experiences that led to it? How can you apply what you've learned to your life in the future? Answering these questions can make the difference between growing better or growing bitter.

 ## Journaling: Major Change and Your Emotions

Reflect on the emotions that followed a major change in your life. What were these emotions and how did you resolve them? If some of these emotions have not been resolved, how have they affected your life since this change took place? What is one step you can take toward healing an unresolved emotion?

EXERCISE

Ritual: Forgiving the Past

Forgiving the person you think "done you wrong" is the key to freedom. Otherwise, we are kept connected to the other person, and the past conditions we are trying to escape continue to affect our current behavior and relationships.

An important part of the ritual of forgiveness is to also forgive ourselves. Sometimes we harbor guilt and regret for our own part in a difficult life event.

Finally, in the following visualization process, we ask the other person to forgive us. This closes the circle.

The Ritual:

1. In a deeply relaxed state, ask your Higher Self to protect and guide this process so that the results may be for the greatest good for all concerned.
2. Imagine the person you want to forgive is standing opposite and directly facing you.
3. Tell the person that you are performing this ritual to release negative thoughts and emotions that keep you connected to him or her in a dysfunctional way.
3. Tell this person that you forgive him or her for anything he or she has consciously or unconsciously done--in this lifetime or in any other--to hurt you. Try to be specific while remembering these hurts.
4. Now, ask the other person to forgive you for any hurts you have caused him or her, consciously or unconsciously, in this lifetime or in any other. Think about what these hurts might specifically be.
5. Bless the other person and tell them they can now leave.
6. Be sure to forgive yourself for any words and behavior related to this person that you now regret.
7. Important: This process should only be done with good will and positive emotion. It is important not to force the other person to do anything to suit your own ends, even in your visualization process, as another person's individuality is sacrosanct.
8. Finally, thank the Higher Self for guiding and protecting you during this process.

The Stages of a Transition

Stage One: The Stage of Endings or Loss

The beginning of a difficult transition involves the experience of things ending. There is usually a profound sense of loss. For example, if you are facing a divorce, you may not only lose a former life partner, but also your social position as a married person, a level of income, perhaps a house, an intact family unit, and if there is a move involved, a familiar living area. You may be experiencing a bitter feud involving money or custody rights. If you are older, you may continue to worry about reentering the dating pool and whether you are still attractive to others. Perhaps being alone is particularly frightening because it sometimes entails loneliness and a feeling of being restless and unsettled in life.

> The beginning stage of a transition is one of loss. Everything that you once identified with may be ripped away. This stage feels like a death. While it is not obvious in the beginning, these circumstances prepare you for a period of deep-seated inner change and a new orientation to life.

In another example, if you have contracted a serious illness, you may have to curtail or quit your current livelihood in order to deal with a schedule of doctors, procedures and prescriptive drugs. This may entail a loss of income as well as a role or position you worked hard to achieve. In addition, you may lose contact with friends or family members who find it difficult to deal with your illness, primarily because it awakens their own fears of mortality. You may lose your mobility or suffer restricted circumstances due to you illness, with a concomitant loss of energy and decreased involvement with social activities. Perhaps you have had to alter your body, such as in breast removal surgery, as a life-saving measure. Handling life change is extraordinarily challenging because of dealing with such losses and the emptiness, confusion, and despair that sometimes follow. Allison's story illustrates how extreme and unexpected changes can demand a new orientation to life:

> Allison was recovering from breast cancer. Prior to dealing with her illness, she was a sales rep for a software company and was known for her aggressive drive and hard-hitting methods. Allison had approached her life with the belief that she was smarter and more competent than most of those around her. But cancer had flattened her, sweeping her right out of her active, demanding life. Initially, she had felt embittered: hadn't she done everything right? She had worked hard and "was a good person." But Allison's dreams showed her that, at 43, she needed to begin using a different approach to life. Far from being a "punishment," her illness was forcing her to see that she couldn't finesse her own way out of her predicament; she had to learn to let go and let God. Allison's competency had served her ego very well; now she needed to surrender to something greater.

Used to actively *calling the shots*, Allison was now forced to enter into a *Neutral Zone* or *Middle Period* to see what life wanted of her. Allison was entering a stage or transition she could not control but could only collaborate with: she was "waiting on the hand of God."

It's important not to ignore or diminish your feelings of loss during this stage. The bromides "What's done is done" or "Let bygones be bygones" do not apply: this period is a natural cycle of mourning that should not be prematurely ended. The end of an old life is like a symbolic death. This symbolic death involves disengagement--removing ourselves from routines and patterns, people and situations associated with a previous way of life. There is also disidentification: once "out of your element," you may begin wondering who you are apart from everything that once defined you. Disenchantment or disillusionment is also involved: we may feel betrayed or let down by people or organizations or by society itself. We realize that things were not what we thought they were. Becoming disillusioned is a way for us to grasp that it's time to move on in life by first revising a former way of thinking. Finally, we experience disorientation: we feel empty and lost. Old fears of death, abandonment, and rejection arise. We are ready to enter into the non-world of Stage Two.

Stage Two: The Middle Stage or Neutral Zone

This stage is sometimes known as the desert period because it feels like a never-ending and apparently fruitless time of wandering, like the Israelites winding through the Sinai Desert for 40 years. Everything old has ended and nothing new has begun. People sometimes compare this stage to *twisting in the wind* or *being hung out to dry*. While it seems that there isn't anything of note happening, this period of time is a gestation or incubation period, when new but hidden creative developments are stirring. Stage Two could be called a time of *fertile emptiness*.

People handle Stage Two in different ways. It's difficult for out-going Americans to be patient with a transition period that cannot be managed with a "Snap out of it" or "Grab the bull by the horns" or "Lean in, power through, and stay tough" approach. This stage cannot be so much managed as cooperated with. As stated earlier, some people decide to try to escape this stage by spending more time in front of the television or computer, increasing their social engagements, burying themselves in daily busy-ness, or self-medicating with drugs or alcohol. At times, people make impulsive decisions to make sudden life changes just to get something going, but decisions made under these conditions usually do not work out.

> The middle stage of a transition is difficult to transit because everything in your former life has ended--and nothing new has yet begun. People sometimes try to cope with this part of the transition cycle by trying to artificially force changes; they can also abort the process altogether. It's important to learn how to use change to re-assess the past in order to better design the future.

There are certain things you can do, however, during this time of suspension and uncertainty. Finding an ally is important, whether the support person is a clergy member, a licensed psychotherapist or a wise and trusted friend. One of the things that can make this time difficult is that most people are not educated about the cycles of change and what they mean. You may feel rejected, misunderstood or criticized by friends and family because they fear or cannot comprehend what you are experiencing. Finding a support system is key to navigating your way when all the usual road signs in life are missing or inadequate. In the following vignette, Michael found beneficial ways to turn his life around.

> Michael felt stuck in the middle period of a divorce. He had not resolved the emotions relating to his ex-wife, such as anger, betrayal, and bitterness. In fact, he tried to bury these emotions by working longer hours, including weekends. He began drinking more, too, until he was faced with his first DUI. It was at this time that Michael began psychotherapy on the recommendation of his lawyer. He learned that he needed to work through his emotions, which included mourning the passing of his marriage. Michael agreed to shorten his working hours, renew his gym membership, and limit his drinking. Most importantly, Michael realized that he needed to find out who he was apart from being a husband, father, and his role at work. Spending time alone hiking and camping in nature seemed to Michael to be a good place to begin looking more deeply at himself.

The middle or neutral stage requires a state of *being* rather than of *doing*. Another way of saying this is that the values of the feminine principle are needed. It is crucial to surrender to this period of apparent emptiness. Behaviors supportive of this approach are those that encourage reflection and introspection, such as:

- dream work
- journaling
- psychotherapy
- reading and writing poetry
- listening to beautiful, soothing music
- spending time reading spiritual scriptures
- walking on the beach or among trees
- gardening
- playing with pets

- taking up yoga or tai chi
- making bean soup
- easel painting or working with clay
- meditation or contemplation
- making an effort to stay silent for 24 hours

These activities allow you to reassess and reevaluate your life, to reprioritize what's important to you, and to more deeply connect to your spiritual center for guidance. These activities cultivate the interior life and develop your inner ear, so that you can hear your Higher Self's counsels. By honoring this stage through the expression of feminine energies-- which encourage transformation, spirituality, and the processes of psychological death and rebirth--you are preparing the way for something new to enter your life.

 *Journaling: Your Middle Zone*

During a transition in your life, what activities did you engage in during the middle or neutral period? Were they attempts to escape your situation, or were they activities that encouraged reflection and introspection? What activity was the most beneficial to you?

___
___
___
___
___
___
___
___
___
___
___

Stage Three: The Stage of Beginnings or Renewal

Eventually, something new appears in your life: unexpectedly, you get a call with a job offer, you meet someone with whom you fall in love, or a windfall of money allows you to move in a new direction. You eventually see a return of your energy and feel a renewed enthusiasm for life. You are not the same, and so life seems different.

> The end stage of a transition is a rebirth, similar to rising up and reclaiming your life. But you have changed, and your outer life reflects this. You begin an active life once again but your perspective has shifted. You may have reprioritized what you think is truly important in life, and you now want to go in a whole new direction: perhaps you want to spend more time with your children, take up a meditation practice, or make a radical change in careers.

If you stay the course, allowing yourself time to resolve unfinished business and to harvest the benefits from your experience, you will grow as a person. Few people understand that suffering through and especially, learning from, change and transition give you more ballast or weight as a person. You are no longer tossed this way or that by the storms of life. Others are more likely to see you as someone who deserves respect and whose opinion is worthy. Experiencing life's tests and trials gives us more inner authority, and other people unconsciously recognize this.

By successfully navigating life's ups and downs, your personal growth shows up in your day-to-day behavior and interactions. You may demonstrate more compassion for others, increased tolerance, greater freedom from what others think of you, and improved stability and strength when facing unexpected situations in your life. You may find that you are now seeking a form of spirituality that allows you to connect to something meaningful, immediate, and real. Finding a means to be of service, whether in big ways or small, may seem of greater importance to you.

EXERCISE
Thinking from the End

1. Imagine that you have SUCCESSFULLY come out the other end of a long, difficult and challenging life passage.
2. Thinking from this end, visualize what you are doing in your life, where you are living, and whom you are with. Most importantly, note how you are feeling about yourself. (Feeling drives the process of manifestation).
3. Make everything as positive as you can and yet remain within the realm of possibility. Try to break down the steps you need to accomplish to achieve such an outcome. (We have to make an effort, as this process is a reciprocal endeavor: Spirit interacts with us when we make sincere efforts to make our lives better).
4. An important part of this process is to ask for a result that embodies the greatest good—after all, something grand that you haven't even thought of may be in the works!
5. Don't forget to be grateful!

In The Next Chapter

In the following chapter, the importance of resilience in successfully meeting change and negotiating transitions will be considered. We will briefly look at what types of people are most resilient and what qualities such a person exhibits. And by the way, just by still being alive (and choosing to read this book), you are already somewhere on the positive end of the resilience scale!

CHAPTER TWO:
Resilience: What It Is, Who Has It, What It Looks Like

Things do not change; we change.

~Henry David Thoreau

*I read and walked for miles at night along the beach,
writing bad blank verse
and searching endlessly for someone wonderful
who would step out of the darkness and change my life.
It never crossed my mind that that person could be me.*

~Anna Quindlen

What is Resilience?

Resilience is an individual's ability to cope with stress and adversity. Other phrases used for psychological resilience are "hardiness," "resourcefulness," and "mental toughness." A person may be able to "bounce back" to where he or she was before the life crisis, without showing any lasting damaging effects. But resilience can also lead to personal growth or to a "bouncing forward," that is gained from dealing with life's inevitable tests and trials. This book is aimed at helping people to not only endure or survive difficult change but to improve, to grow, and to thrive!

Who is Resilient?

Much of the initial research on resilience had to do with studies of invulnerable or invincible children. These were children born and reared in chronic poverty, most with absent or psychologically disturbed parents, many living in drug-infested or crime-ridden neighborhoods. Yet, some of these children developed into competent adults who maintained stable jobs and long-term relationships. They were considered invulnerable to the detrimental circumstances into which they were born or raised. Studies of these children have been conducted with the focus on what qualities allowed them to surmount their surroundings to lead productive lives. Researchers reported that the most important factor in their success was the cultivation of supportive positive relationships, either inside or outside the family. Somehow, these children found at least one adult who could provide encouragement and caring, who could mentor them and model positive adult behaviors.

> Factors such as age, outlook, and personal history of traumatic events influence how well individuals deal with crises. Researchers have studied children who thrive in the face of crime, deprivation and mental illness, prisoners of war and combat soldiers who manage to remain resilient, and even the neural pathways and brain chemicals that may play a part in resilient behavior.

In addition to studies of invulnerable children, resilience has been explored in diverse settings and under various conditions. For example, researchers have observed survivors of extended periods of internment in Nazi concentration or POW camps to find out what psychological qualities made them resilient. There is research that credits prisoner survival to progressive coping skills (in contrast to regressive, passive behavior or a submissive approach). Progressive coping includes the ability to analyze situations, to take protective action in the face of possible danger, and to improve personal circumstances whenever possible.

In recent years, scientists have focused on locating neural circuits and brain chemicals that help individuals survive high levels of stress while remaining highly functional. Facing manageable stressors during childhood ("stress inoculation") appears to reduce negative behavioral and hormonal responses to stress later in life.

Research has found that cultivating an optimistic attitude, positively reframing the meaning of a negative situation, being open to social support, and maintaining spiritual beliefs and practices all involve specific molecular adaptations, neurobiological mechanisms, and the activation of brain reward circuits that contribute to resiliency.

In another development in the field of resiliency study, researchers in various institutes around the world are investigating ways to help people prepare for catastrophes and to become more resilient should they face large-scale disasters such as hurricanes and earthquakes. The development of resilience in individuals may be generally applicable to widespread situations--such as disease pandemics, wars, or natural disasters--that compromise interdependent systems, both locally and globally. Preparing a large population for a widespread calamity will require an integration of theories in human resilience with ideas from the fields of communication, disaster planning, ecology, engineering, public health, and computing.

Currently, studies of resilience in individuals regard resilience as much more than mere coping skills in the face of adversity. Resilience includes learning the skills needed to be emotionally strong, proactive, and decisive. Resilience is demonstrated by the ability to communicate well and to form long-lasting relationships. Today, resilience involves prevention. Resilience can help you excel in all areas of life--the work place, romantic relationships, and family.

Quiz: How Much Do You Know About Resilience?

Choose and circle what you think is the correct answer among the choices for each question below: (Answers are given at the end of the quiz questions).[1]

1. In general, which group shows the greatest resilience?
A. Children
B. Teens
C. Adults
D. Women
E. Men

2. In general, which group shows the least resilience?
A. Grieving people
B. Insecure people
C. Quick-tempered people
D. Self-involved people
E. Unstable people

3. Under which circumstances is it most difficult to be resilient?
A. After natural disasters such as hurricanes and earthquakes
B. After events over which a person appears not to have control, such as an accident
C. After events that connect to earlier trauma, such as childhood sexual or physical abuse
D. After events involving bodily harm or injury
E. After experiencing traumatic events in a foreign country

---

[1] These items were paraphrased from the more comprehensive WebMD quiz: "Stress Management: How Resilient Are You?" at http://www.webmd.com/balance/stress-management/resilience-quiz.

4. Which of these qualities are characteristic of resilient people?
A. Interdependence
B. Perseverance
C. Empathy
D. Intuition
E. All of the above

5. Which is a true statement regarding resilient people?
A. When faced with difficulties, they are more immune to stress than the average person
B. In times of turmoil and stress, they are willing to reach out to trained professionals for help
C. They can easily bury, compartmentalize or suppress unpleasant events in their lives
D. They are more likely to have earned a cardiopulmonary resuscitation (CPR) certification or to be trained as an emergency First Responder.
E. They tend to have positive, supportive parents and a happy childhood.

Answers:

1. A-Children. When we are adults, the world seems a certain way, and when everything falls apart, we are often shattered. Even though children can feel frightened and vulnerable in the face of change, they have not yet had the opportunity to construct a fully formed idea of the world. Their egos have not fully formed and so they are more open to change. Both of these factors allow them to be more flexible when disaster strikes.

In the invulnerable children studies, these children are described as abused, neglected, and mistreated, with parents who are criminals, addicts or mentally ill. The studies report that about one-third of the children grow up to lead successful and well-adjusted lives, without crippling emotional and psychological problems.

2. D-Self-Involved people. Egocentric or self-involved people are less objective and more subjective, and often exhibit less emotional intelligence or self-awareness. Taking things personally affects their ability to be resilient. You probably know someone who makes big drama out of every trauma--even when to others the trauma seems self-made and less than urgent. It is the meaning we put on events that makes it possible for us to problem-solve, to cope and adapt--and this means being able to detach enough from a sudden and difficult change to see it as a natural part of human life and experience.

3. C-Events connected to an older trauma. If an event connects to an older childhood trauma--a trauma for which we didn't have the ego strength or intellectual maturity to deal with at the time--the pain that is triggered can be so much greater because of all it dredges up. This is a crucial time to work with a psychotherapist or other trained professional to help recognize and name this trauma; you do not have to remain a victim of your past. My formula is: When the pain of staying the same is greater than the fear of change, people will usually seek the help they need!

4. E-All of the above. Resilient people show both independence and reliance on others: they are interdependent. They are able to maintain healthy boundaries in the face of trauma but they can ask for help from others when they feel a need. They have a firm sense of values and of their self-worth, but they do not take life so seriously that they fail to see the humor in everyday events. They have insight about their strengths and weaknesses and can admit to their role in the difficulties they are facing.

5. B-Seek help from professionals during difficult times. It is important to know that you can hurt and rebound at the same time! Resilient people recognize that difficult times sometimes call for a more objective perspective from a trained professional or other reliable people. Everyone needs support to help them process and eventually resolve hurt and disappointment. Resilient people know that it is a measure of strength to reach out to others to gain clarity and insight during difficult times.

Qualities of Resilient People

Resilient people do not "walk between the raindrops." They do not deny or bury their difficulties. Neither are they perfectly equipped to handle every crisis that comes their way. What resilient people do have is perspective: they recognize that crises are part of life, and that it is possible to learn greater resourcefulness, stamina, and confidence in the face of calamities. And they are not afraid to seek out others who are trained to help them navigate challenging times. The following are qualities that characterize resilience. You may already exhibit many of these qualities to some degree or another; they can all be increased and enhanced with greater awareness and practice.

> Resilient people are not an exclusive or special breed of people. Everyone is already resilient in some cases and to some degree. Choose qualities from this list that you want to improve upon: perhaps you want to learn from your experiences by exploring them with someone you trust, or you would like to become more flexible and less judgmental by becoming more aware of your rigidities and fears.

1. They learn from experience. Resilient people can reflect on an experience without devastating self-judgment or paralyzing self-criticism. They want to find the "take aways" from their traumatic experience to apply to their daily lives.

2. They can laugh at themselves. When resilient people laugh at themselves and the world, things are brought into perspective. This is the idea behind laughter yoga! Laughter strengthens the immune system, relieves stress and depression, and fosters creativity. It has been scientifically proven that the cardio workout from ten minutes of hearty laughter is equal to thirty minutes on a rowing machine. We can all share a chuckle at the wit of actress Helen Hayes, who at 73, quipped that "The hardest years in life are those between ten and seventy."

3. They are flexible. They are serious and humorous, self-confident and self-critical, optimistic and pessimistic. They embody opposite traits at the same time, which allows them to respond in various ways to life events. They are not all-or-nothing, black-and-white personalities. Persons with emotional flexibility are able to express their emotions at the right time and in the appropriate way.

4. They are solution-oriented. They avoid seeing crises as insurmountable. They are good trouble-shooters and problem-solvers. They realize there is more than one solution to a problem, and that working together synergistically with others often produces better results than working alone.

5. They are inter-dependent. They are neither independent nor dependent, but interdependent. Interdependence means resilient people are self-reliant, yet they can reach out to make connections to a few reliable others for support.

6. They have empathy for others. Sympathy can often serve as a way of enabling others in an unhealthy way, whereas empathy is encouraging others in a strengthening way. People who have developed empathy are able to listen to and understand what others are experiencing. They often make use of pattern empathy, that is, they can enter a room and immediately get a sense of the room's emotional "climate." This awareness is also known as emotional intelligence, and gives persons with high empathy a sense of good timing--they are able to spot early clues or hidden agendas in the business organization or social group to which they belong.

7. They show perseverance. Resilient people keep going in the face of disappointment, discouragement and apparent failure. Winston Churchill once urged a group of students, "Never, ever, ever, ever, ever, ever, ever, give up. Never give up. Never give up. Never give up." Setting realistic goals and then successfully attaining them helps to build stamina and confidence to draw on when things get tough.

8. They use intuition, creativity, and imagination. Intuition is the ability to receive information from the unconscious. Resilient people learn to rely on clues or hunches during daily life and to utilize information from their nightly dreams. Some people seem naturally intuitive, but this quality can be fostered in anyone. Intuition can be enhanced most directly by learning how to remember, record, and interpret dreams. Resilient people can problem-solve in novel ways because they see unusual connections, which is sometimes called creative competence. Such people are open-brained and non-judgmental. There is a practical component needed to make the most of these qualities: ideas from the unconscious must be made physically manifest to be of use to the world. This can be done best when we have "our heads in the clouds and our feet on the ground."

9. They develop an inner life. They look for opportunities for self-discovery, such as engaging in journal writing, dream work, reading spiritually-oriented books, or taking up meditation. Such activities provide inner resources when times get tough. Cultivating an inner life means being able to sustain aloneness, or coming home to oneself. Most importantly, developing an inner life helps a person formulate a broad sense of meaning and purpose in life, which makes it possible to see challenges in greater perspective.

 *Journaling: Your Qualities of Resilience*

Review the qualities of resilient people that are briefly outlined above. On the lines below, list below those qualities that you think are most characteristic of you, with an example of how you have applied each quality to a specific situation in your life.

 *Journaling: Qualities to Strengthen*

What quality or qualities do you feel are lacking or are under-developed in your character? Which qualities would you like to strengthen? Write down any instances you can remember when a weak quality proved to be a liability in your life.

# *Check List: Rate Your Resilience Quotient*

The folowing list of qualities are considered a good measure of how resilient you are! Use "O" to rate qualities you believe you have developed to an outstanding degree. Use "A" to rate those qualities you judge to be at an average level of development. Mark with an "S" those qualities you think require strengthening.

_____**1. Persistence:** You do not easily give up when faced with a problem or obstacle in life.

_____**2. Flexibility:** You are able to easily change your behavior if you see that you are heading in the wrong direction or that your solution to an issue/problem is not working.

_____**3. Humor:** You are able to see the irony or humor in situations, which helps you put your difficulties into perspective.

_____**4. Optimism:** You believe that your current troubles will eventually end and that all will be well.

_____**5. Interdependence:** You have a social circle of support that you can depend on and to which you offer assistance in turn.

_____**6. Perceptiveness:** You have insight into people and situations, and you can make up your own mind about what you see or hear.

_____**7. Self-Motivation:** You find the drive to achieve your goals and you have the ability to act on your own.

_____**8. Service:** You invest time and money into those people or causes in which you believe.

_____**9. Creativity:** You are resourceful and imaginative and can express yourself with originality and inspiration.

_____**10: Ethics:** You follow your conscience so that your decisions are made with the highest good of others in mind.

_____**11. Empathy:** You can easily "walk in others' shoes" and understand without judgment why they might think or behave in a certain way.

_____**12. Spirituality:** You acknowledge something greater than yourself, a sense of source that gives your life purpose and meaning.

Persistence and Flexibility

Two qualities necessary to becoming more resilient deserve special attention. Psychologist Paul T. P. Wong asserts that the two most important life strategies essential to survival and resilience are persistence and flexibility. These are the traits common to both successful CEOs and athletes. Dr. Wong quotes Calvin Coolidge, the 30th President of the United States, who famously stated:

> Maintaining focus and determination toward a goal and a willingness to "pivot" to a new viewpoint and approach when it is needed, is the secret to survival and resilience!

Nothing in the
world can take the place of persistence.
Talent will not;
Genius will not;
Education will not;
Persistence and determination alone are omnipotent.

Wong's research shows that if pain and fear can be overcome in one difficult situation, the optimism learned in surmounting that difficulty can then be generalized and applied to other challenging situations. Learned resilience and generalized persistence, Wong attests, along with flexibility--or agility and creativity--are equally necessary to manage life's crises. Persistence without flexibility may result in short-sighted or misguided behavior; flexibility without persistence can become weakness. In short, true persistence is flexible!

In life, what does the partnership of these two qualities look like? When you face an obstacle with persistence, it's not about repeatedly banging your head against the wall. After carefully thinking your situation over, be ready to *pivot* your point-of-view and to try different things to see what will work. If one particular approach doesn't work, keep trying different ways of coming at the issue until you find the right strategy. When you find your path is blocked by a stone wall, don't go through it: go under, around, or over it to get to the other side. This is flexible perseverance or persistent flexibility!

In The Next Chapter
Chapter Three will take a look at how we can remove self-created roadblocks to resiliency, such as habitually responding to situations with excess stress (distress), inhibiting fears, or placating behaviors. This chapter presents practical ways to become more aware of these behaviors and to modify or change them to boost resiliency. Suggestions for removing blocks include learning to take more risks, using humor to lift your mood, and even changing undesirable behaviors through active imagination! Sharpen your pencil for the interactive journaling and exercises ahead!

CHAPTER THREE:
Removing Blocks to Resilience

*Change will never happen when people lack the ability
and courage to see themselves for who they are.*

~Bryant H. McGill

If you do not change direction, you may end up where you are heading.

~Lao Tzu

There are certain emotional responses and patterns of behavior that block resilience in the face of change. All of us have developed patterns that at some point we must correct or outgrow; some of these patterns were learned in childhood as ways to cope with difficult circumstances and some were simply modeled after an adult in our environment. Reducing damaging stress, lessening incapacitating fears and modifying perfectionistic tendencies improve your ability to manage change. This chapter gives you practical strategies to apply to your daily life. You will learn ways to *self-correct* or modify your behaviors so that you are not at the mercy of life's sudden and unpredictable events!

BLOCK #1: EXCESSIVE STRESS

De-Stress: Set Your Burdens Down...

Someone once sent the following anonymously written story to me, which I took the liberty of rewriting.

A woman walked around the room while holding a glass of water. As the main seminar speaker, she was presenting ways to relieve and manage stress. The audience was expecting her to ask the age old question, "Is the glass half-empty of half-full?" But she fooled them all.

> While some degree of stress is necessary for living daily life, intense, prolonged stress may create anxiety, headaches, high blood pressure, and reactive behaviors such as excessive anger and nervous reactions. The following section discusses ways to manage the inevitable stressors of life.

With a smile she asked, "How heavy is the glass of water?" Answers from the audience ranged from 8 to 20 ounces. She responded, "The actual weight of the glass doesn't matter, because the *weight depends on how long you hold the glass*." She continued, "If I hold it for an hour, my right arm will begin to ache. And if I hold it for a day, someone will need to call an ambulance. In each case, it's the same weight, but the longer I hold it, the heavier it becomes."

The speaker concluded, "And that's the way it is with stress. If we carry our bundle of burdens all the time, it will become increasingly heavy. She put down the glass of water on the podium. "We have to set our burdens down for a while in order to rest and recuperate. When we're refreshed, we can carry on."

Life is naturally stressful, both at home and at work. At home, the needs of your spouse and your children, budgetary concerns, pet care, home maintenance and other demands contribute to your burden of stress. Work stressors include lay-offs, organizational changes, downsizing, and professional relationships. You can measure your level of stress by recognizing certain symptoms: sleep problems, over-eating or loss of appetite, over-medicating with alcohol, prescription or recreational drugs, reduced energy, and arriving late for work or meetings.

Stress Busters

Below is a list of stress busters to help you manage your stress quotient! Look through the list below and choose only one or two to work on at any one time.

- **Breathe deeply!** Practice diaphragmatic breathing by putting one hand on your stomach and another on your chest. As you slowly breathe in through your nose, the hand on your chest should drop and the hand on your stomach should rise. As you slowly breathe out through your mouth, the hand on your stomach should now drop and the hand on your chest remain the same.

- **Don't overdo your "to do" list!** Set priorities and only try to accomplish the most important items.

- **Reframe your thoughts.** When you catch yourself thinking negatively about yourself or your situation, edit your thoughts! Instead of thinking, "I am terrible at being interviewed," say "I practiced, so I will do the best I can!"

- **Take a mid-day walk.** When things seem over-whelming, try to get outside for a walk during lunch or shortly after work. If you can, try to get to the gym a few times a week.

- **Journal.** Writing your thoughts down in a journal helps to release worrisome thoughts and bottled-up emotions.

- **Pray or meditate.** Spend time connecting to your spiritual source. This brings peace and balance to your life.

- **Have hobbies or interests.** Take up modeling with clay or woodworking. Do something that serves as a creative outlet in your life.

- **Talk to someone.** Share your day with someone you trust, someone who will not judge you or give you unsolicited advice.

- **Hug a child or play with a pet.** Children and animals offer us unconditional love.

- **Volunteer.** Helping others puts your own problems in perspective.

- **Read or listen to something humorous.** Watch a funny movie or read a humorous book! (A few funny one-liners are offered below).

Humor Helps!

As we mentioned in our earlier discussion of laughter yoga, we know that humor relaxes tension. Here's a few humorous lines to lift your spirits!

- Accept the fact that some days you're the pigeon, and other days you're the statue!

- Keep your words soft and sweet, in case you have to eat them.

- If you can't be kind, at least have the decency to be vague.

- It may be your sole purpose in life is to serve as a warning to others.

- When everything is coming your way, you're in the wrong lane.

- Never put both feet in your mouth at the same time or you won't have a leg to stand on.

 *Journaling: Reducing Your Stress*

What situations create stress in your life?
___
___
___
___

Choose one of the above tips to reduce stress to apply to your life and tell how you implemented or will implement this strategy. Try it for three weeks, the time it takes to create a new habit.
___
___
___
___

Write about using this tip, or any other, to successfully handle a formerly stressful situation.
___
___
___
___
___
___
___
___
___

BLOCK #2: OVERWHELMING FEARS

Even the most confident persons you know have fears. Fear prevents people from embracing change. Fear "freezes" you in position, which stops you from being creative, taking risks, or learning from experiences. Fear prevents resilience. The following sections will help you learn how to identify your fears and to deal with them by taking greater risks in your life.

> Fear can be felt anywhere along a continuum, from a vague uneasiness to a full-blown panic. Mastering fear means to let go of worrying about the future or ruminating about the past. Try saying to yourself, "I have done all I can, now I let this go," or repeating the phrase, "I let go and let God."

 *Journaling: Dealing With Fear*

1. Name your greatest fear. Staring your fear in the face can reduce its power over you and melt it away just like the watery demise of the Wicked Witch of the East in *The Wizard of Oz*. You can throw cold water on your fear with the realization that you can and will survive the coming change in your life.

_____
_____
_____
_____
_____
_____
_____
_____
_____
_____

2. Imagine this fear coming true. What do you feel? How would you handle this worst-case scenario? (Knowing you can manage whatever happens reduces fear and increases your confidence).

_____

_____

_____

_____

_____

3. Don't worry! Research shows that 90% of what we worry about never happens. Have there been times when you have worried about something that did *not* happen? How can you change this pattern of worry?

_____

_____

_____

_____

_____

4. Revisit the past. Remember a time when you successfully navigated a change and transition period. It may have been difficult but you now realize this time of turmoil eventually brought new opportunities and better conditions into your life. Are there any pointers you could give yourself to help you in your current situation? What beneficial attitudes and actions used in the previous situation can you now apply to your present challenge?

_____

_____

_____

_____

_____

5. Get busy! Be proactive by finding something you can do about your situation. This lessens fear and helps you to feel more in control. If you have a feeling that you might lose your job in the next few months, for example, you can reduce your anticipatory fear by exploring job search engines on the Internet, talking to your network of business contacts, and updating your resume. Discuss one

_____

_____

_____

_____

_____

action item you can accomplish to help you deal with your fear.

6. Be positive. When you catch a negative, self-critical thought, stop it from completely forming. You do not have to accept these thoughts! Repel them and counter them with positive, self-supportive thoughts. Create affirmations with which to replace these negative thoughts, such as "I am conquering my fears," "I am able to successfully handle change," or "I am becoming more confident daily." Write a few affirmations of your own on the lines below:

_____

_____

_____

_____

_____

7. Find support. It's a sign of strength to ask for help when you need it. Your support network can include family members, colleagues, mentors, mental health professionals, clergy, and friends. Write down the members of your current support team and anyone you would like to add to this team in the future:

_____

_____

_____

_____

_____

An important antidote to fear is learning to take risks. There are Type T, or *thrill*-seeking, personalities who crave novelty and excitement. Most of us, however, learn to take risks by building on small successes over time. Taking risks allows us to face change and transition with a sense of adventure, even in the face of discomfort. The exercise below will help you explore your risk taking options!

Learning to Take Risks

Risks in life are unavoidable: committing to a relationship, investing in a business, changing careers, booking a flight when you are afraid to fly. Your willingness to take risks is related to how easily you handle change. The good news is that you can prepare yourself to manage risks with more flexibility and resiliency. In fact, you can actually learn to take calculated risks to advance your goals and enrich your life. It helps you to grow if you push your risk limits beyond what you feel is comfortable. Taking risks helps you to better negotiate change and transition.

> Risk-taking behavior can be as small as deciding to take a new gym class and as large as starting your own business. Everyone has a different capacity for embarking on something new--the key element is getting past fear.

In the exercise below, you will put risk-taking behavior into action. You are creating the courage to change through practice! The instructions for this exercise encourage you to report the results of having taken a small risk in some area of your life. Be careful not to try too many risks in too many areas at once! And of course, be practical in how you choose and then execute these risks. In addition, be sure to look at any risks that "fail" as an experiment that taught you a valuable lesson.

 ## *Journaling: Six Areas of Life*

Look at six areas of your life: home, relationships, personal, finances, work, spirituality. Choose a small risk to take in each area. For each life area specified below, describe this small risk and in the additional space, write what results occurred as a result of taking the risk. The first two areas include examples to get you started!

Home: Example: Clear our clutter from closets and/or garage. You will feel freer, and creating space allows something new to come into your life. Write one risk you intend to take on the home-front on the following lines:

___

What were the results of having taken this risk?

___

Relationships: Example: Write to someone with whom you have a sense of unfinished business. It's better to actually write a postal letter than to email or text, as you want to create closure with thoughtful, well-expressed thoughts and feelings. Try to leave out resentment or accusations. Write one risk you will take in the area of relationships on the following lines:

___

What were the results of having taken this risk?

___

Personal: Write one risk you intend to take in your personal life (examples would be joining an online dating service, embarking on a weight-loss program, or taking up knitting).

_____
_____
_____
_____

What were the results of having taken this risk?

_____
_____
_____
_____

Finances: Write one risk you intend to take in the area of finances:

_____
_____
_____
_____

What were the results of having taken this risk?

_____
_____
_____
_____

Work: Write one risk you intend to take relating to your job:

_____
_____
_____
_____

What were the results of having taken this risk?

_____
_____
_____
_____
_____
_____
_____

Spirituality: Write one risk you intend to take in your spiritual life:

What were the results of having taken this risk?

_____
_____
_____
_____

BLOCK #3: PLACATING BEHAVIOR

Saying Adios to the "Pleaser"

The *pleaser* is someone who attempts to anticipate and meet the needs of others before his or her own. Many of us were raised in families in which we were not able to truly be ourselves. As a result, instead of developing a strong inner center--or personal core of identity within ourselves--we have learned to look *outward* to make sure that our behavior,

> Being a pleaser can often be equated with "selling yourself down the river." Not only do you drown out your own needs but you may not be in touch with all parts of yourself, making it impossible to grow into wholeness.

opinions, and decisions satisfy others. The problem with being a pleaser is that, in the end, we do not make ourselves--or others--very happy. This approach to life makes a person fearful and rigid, just the opposite of being flexible and resilient.

> Alex came to see me because he had recently divorced after 17 years of marriage and had quickly found himself in another relationship. Out of convenience, the couple had decided that his girlfriend would move in with him. Her expectations were high that Alex would marry her. Alex began therapy because he was having misgivings about becoming seriously involved so soon after his divorce. Alex knew that he was a "rescuer" and a "pleaser," and that these co-dependent traits had kept him over-long in an unhappy marriage. When we examined his dreams, we saw that they were repeatedly showing him that he was moving too fast, and that he was in danger of making a poor relationship choice. Alex was hesitant to face an ending to another relationship. But he knew that, in order to be happy, he needed to listen to himself and to risk "displeasing" another person.

Our "Other Side"

If we act out only our "good" side to please others, we are usually out of touch with the "bad child" part of our human nature. In our effort to always appear "perfect" or "good," we lose touch with our innate, instinctual responses to life. At her Tamalpais Institute in Marin County, California, dancer and choreographer Anna Halprin conducts workshops that explore the healing power of dance. Halprin has participants "dance" to their own portraits, first to the pleasant, agreeable presentation of themselves and then to their "other side"--the side that is hidden, wild, untamed, or aggressive. She urges her dancers to acknowledge both sides of themselves as a vital step toward wholeness and healing.[1]

Without a healthy acceptance of our "other side," we may find ourselves lacking appropriate personal boundaries and allowing ourselves to be exploited or victimized. When we are "too nice," the darker aspects of our nature are forced into the unconscious; then we do and say things that we remain largely unaware of but that upset and hurt others. We also see our faults in others: we complain that a friend is petty, a brother is selfish, the boss is tyrannical, a parent is controlling. While there may be some truth to these criticisms, we do not always have the insight to *first locate these traits within ourselves.*

Why should we be familiar with what has been called the "shadow" part of ourselves? One reason is that we do less harm when we know how capable we are of doling it out. And if we are aware of what *we* are capable of, then we can more easily *read* others, perceiving them and our circumstances more realistically. Another reason is that we need the strength of the rejected parts of ourselves; we need to work on modifying the harmfulness of our more negative traits, of course, but this part of our nature can also protect us. The shadow is where we find the anger and aggression and other energies that we can use to appropriately defend ourselves. Being in contact with this part of ourselves allows us to firmly say "No" to someone and to create and maintain healthy boundaries. In order to be flexible and resilient, we need to recognize *all* of our nature; exclusion of any part prevents us from responding in appropriate ways when we run into difficult situations.

Journaling: Getting in Touch With Your "Pleaser Self"

Are you ready to better understand the part of yourself that wants to please no matter what? Work with the questions below to help you recognize this part of yourself and to determine when in your childhood this behavior began.

1. In what way do you find yourself saying "yes" when you want to say "no"? Or when do you find yourself doing things you do not really want to do to avoid upsetting someone?
2. What emotions come up inside of you when you are doing or saying things only to please others? Where in your body do these emotions occur? (For example, some pleasers feel anxiety in the solar plexus area, where our sense of personal power is centered).

3. Write down any memories from childhood that may have conditioned you to react to others in a placating way in order to head off something unpleasant from occurring?

_____
_____
_____
_____
_____
_____
_____
_____

EXERCISE #1

Transforming the "Pleaser Self"

1. In a relaxed state, imagine that you see a younger "you," a child who represents the part of yourself who needs to please.
2. Take the "pleaser" self onto your lap and talk soothingly to the child, telling him or her what you have learned since becoming an adult. Share what you now understand about the importance of speaking from your own center.
3. Ease the child's fears. Encourage the child's sense of well-being. Support the child's sense of identity and self-esteem.
4. Believe it or not, you can actually influence how you feel about yourself, others and life in the present when you return to your childhood in your imagination to replace the perspective of your child-self with a more mature viewpoint.

EXERCISE #2

Standing Your Ground

1. In a related exercise, return to times when you were a child or young adult when you found yourself trying to please others to prevent disapproval, censure, or even violence.
2. What if you re-imagined these past scenes differently? Close your eyes and imagine that during these events, you are able to speak or act in your own behalf.
3. You calmly state what your needs are and what you wish to do or not do.
4. Get in tune with your body so you are aware of how it feels to honor your view-point and to take a stand.

In The Next Chapter
You know that you need resilience to effectively meet life's challenges, and you even know some characteristics of resilience--but what are some practical ways to develop and nurture this quality? In the following chapter, we will explore together a few tools to help you better meet life's changes and transitions. These tools will give you the means to meet change and transition with confidence and certainty.

CHAPTER FOUR:
Building Resilience: Tools for Change

We are products of our past, but we don't have to be prisoners of it.

~Rick Warren

Bending beats breaking.

~Betty Greene

In this chapter, we will look at concepts, exercises, and practices--or tools for change--that will help you apply what you are learning about navigating change and transition to your everyday life. These tweaks and twists to your habitual way of doing things can add excitement and creativity to your life!

TOOL #1: TUNE INTO YOUR DREAMS

Dreams Light the Way

The Middle Zone of a long transition can be described as a time when persons can no longer find road maps or signs to direct their passage through life. The previous life cycle has ended, and the new stage of life has yet to begin. When you feel as if your boat is stuck in the windless sea (which is actually called the *doldrums* in nautical terms), you can rely on dreams to give you an idea of your bearings.

> **Improve Your Dream Recall:** Having a strong desire to remember your dreams is the most important factor in improving your recall. It is also important to relax before bedtime, while repeating to yourself that you will remember a dream. Keep a pen and tablet within easy reach to immediately write down anything, no matter how trivial, that you may recall during the night or in the morning.

Dreams Bring Clarity

Dreams can help us see the possibilities of the future, which is especially important when we wonder if we still have one! During a long stretch of stasis, when life seems without prospects and all we do seems fruitless, our dreams can come to encourage us, enlighten us, and to give us courage to live another day.[2]

> Mary was devastated when her coaching business tanked. She had invested all of her money, time, and energy into her career. She had even moved to a new location where she felt her business would be likelier to flourish. After experiencing one disappointment after another, Mary went into a deep funk and began psychotherapy. Mary soon realized she was being called to revisit her childhood, as she had cut herself off from nearly all early memories. She had to find her roots and learn the reason why she her childhood had been closeted away.

Eventually, after many months of work in psychotherapy, Mary found herself in a long, flat time of introspection, evaluation, and deliberation. For weeks, even her dream life seemed to temporarily dry up. Mary made arrangements to spend five days in a summer vacation rental. Without the distraction of her job, relationship, or daily routine, Mary hoped that her emotions, thoughts and dreams could rise to the surface of consciousness. It was during this time that Mary had the following dream:

In her dream, Mary slowly climbed up a very steep path. She knew she was on the slope of a mountain but she was not able to see its lofty peak, which was obscured by a cover of clouds. At one point in her climb, she came to a wide, grassy meadow, where she rested in the sunlight. She seemed to stay here a long time and was kept company by an occasional visit by a bird, a deer or a rabbit. Mary somehow knew her needs would be met, even though her long and arduous journey was just beginning. Her destination was the mountain's summit, and it might take a lifetime to arrive there.

Mary's dream reassured her that she was making progress in her psychotherapy; she was on her rightful life path, which was a spiritual one (her steep climb up a mountain). She was in a place (the meadow) where nothing seemed to be happening in her life. However, her dream communicated to her that she was being helped (animal friends), and that her needs would be met along the way. Mary needed to trust her process and to cultivate patience; she was truly *waiting on the hand of God*.

Try the following dream exercise to help you figure out what is needed from you in a situation that seems stalled or immobile:

EXERCISE

Dream a Little Dream

1. Get very relaxed, perhaps by first soaking in a hot bath. Find a comfortable, quiet place where you can close your eyes without interruption. Feel yourself become calm and centered. Then ask God, your inner guidance, or your spiritual guide, "What is the most important change I need to make at this time?" or "What is my next step in life?" or perhaps, "What is no longer working in my life?"

2. Be very quiet and allow an image; a word, phrase or sentence; or a sudden understanding come to you. (I often hear song lyrics that exactly fit the bill!) You may hear or see something that brings an answer you did not expect. Write on a tablet or in a journal about your experience.

3. Now, ask for a dream to help you better understand your answer. Before you take your next step or make a change of some sort, request that you would like a dream to help you see why this move is necessary or how it will bring improvements to your life. Be sure to write about this dream in a notebook or journal. Include any emotions you felt in the dream or upon awakening. Write how this dream has brought greater understanding or clarity to your life.

TOOL #2: TRY JOURNALING

Partnering with Life

Why is it important to keep a journal? Keeping a journal is a way of collaborating with life. You become more aware of the cycles and patterns and rhythms in your life. Journaling is a way of becoming conscious of the deeper meaning underlying everyday events. I've heard people say that, until they had actually written down their thoughts and feelings about a topic, they had not really known where they had stood! When you journal, you are declaring that you are open to change. Journaling helps you process your experiences so that you can more easily and quickly complete transitions to move forward in life.

For example, if you write how you truly feel about your current job, you may realize that it's important for you to move on to something new, to an area of fresh activity that can help you grow and thrive.

It's important not to get hung up by how to record your thoughts: you can use your cell phone's note function, you can speak into a recorder, or you can keep an on-going journal on your laptop. Some people keep their daily journal writings as well as their dreams in the same notebook journal; others record dreams in one place and keep their daily journal entries in another. What is important is the consistency with which you journal.

> Journaling is most effective if you can do it once or twice a week for about 20 minutes (make a "date" with your journal). It doesn't matter where you begin, and it sometimes helps to simply write down your "stream of consciousness," forgetting spelling and punctuation rules for an easier flow. This bypasses the mental "censor." Privacy is important. You can choose a theme for a period of time (some journals come with themes or "writing prompts" included). Think freedom of expression!

When, or how often, you journal is significant because making regular entries helps to develop your relationship with yourself as well as your inner guidance. Setting aside time at least once or twice a week is important. At the beginning of each new month, I love to go back through my journal to review the dreams and journal entries for the same month for the previous two to three years. This is useful because we sometimes find ourselves living another turn on the spiral, or experiencing similar events or concerns from perhaps a slightly different perspective at the same time each year!

Now, what goes into your journal? Whatever you want! You can include your uncensored thoughts, your deepest emotions, and questions about your life, your goals, wishes, and affirmations. You can write a letter to someone (that may never be sent) to get closure to a situation or to express emotions that need releasing. You can also fill the journal with your poems, songs, illustrations, comments, opinions, lists and concerns. I occasionally find an online picture or photo of something or someone that is in one of my dreams and paste it into my journal. Being creative brings your journal *alive* and makes your journal a partner in life.

Benefits of Journaling

Some researchers claim that journaling has a positive impact on physical well-being. University of Texas (Austin) psychologist James Pennebaker asserts that regular journaling helps persons come to terms with stressful events, which not only relieves stress but can actually strengthen the immune system. Other research indicates that consistent journal writing can decrease the symptoms of asthma (Louise Hay, author of *You Can Heal Your Life*, associates asthma with feeling stifled or with suppressed crying) and rheumatoid arthritis (which may be related to victimization, resentment, bitterness).

Additional benefits of journaling come from the field of brain research. When you write, you are utilizing your left-brain, or the analytic and rational, part of your brain. This frees the intuitive, feeling and creative part of your brain, or the right side, so that you are using both sides of your brain to help you better understand yourself and your life.

> **Journaling brings benefits to both your psychological and physical health and well-being. The act of writing about your problems relieves stress, promotes problem-solving, and helps you to learn about yourself!**

In summary, journaling brings the following benefits into your life:

- **Clearly see your thoughts and feelings.** Writing things down takes thoughts out of the "air" where they may seem vague or confusing and "earths" or solidifies them. Your thoughts and feelings become better organized and are clarified for you.

- **Relieve stress.** Writing about why you are experiencing emotions (preferably while you are experiencing them) such as anger, fear, and sadness will help to release or reduce them. As you write, it will also help you to see the stress-producing situation from all angles, which enables you to become more objective. You might even be able to pinpoint the childhood family pattern that still influences you to react in certain ways, which leads you to:

- **Get to know yourself.** Writing on a regular basis will help you learn what situations and people are unhealthy for you. You will more clearly see what things make you happy so that your goals become more defined. You will also begin to get in touch with something that seems solid and sacred, sometimes called a spiritual center, that offers reliable guidance and has your overall well-being in mind.

- **Use your journal for conflict-resolution.** Work out problems and issues with others in your journal before you have a verbal argument that cannot be mended. Try to see the argument from all sides and do your best to come to a compromise or solution. This exercise can save a lot of wear and tear on both personal and professional relationships!

- **Track your progress.** Keeping a journal over time makes it possible for you to track your growth and progress. You can see what your concerns have been in the past and how you have handled them. When you face current troubles, you can review your journal to gain confidence from having successfully navigated through difficult changes and transitions in the past.

A Gratitude Journal

If there are psychological and physical benefits to keeping a journal, regularly jotting down what you are thankful for may be even more advantageous. Researchers list better sleep, fewer illnesses, and greater happiness as a few of the positive results of keeping a gratitude journal. Robert Emmons, a professor at the University of California (Davis) and a well-known expert in the science of gratitude, offers the following research-based tips for getting the most out of practicing gratitude:

> **Writing down the things you are grateful for enhances a sense of well-being, increases compassion for others, and importantly, invites more blessings into your life. You do not have to do this daily; in fact, writing what you are thankful for is more effective if done about once or twice a week. You could actually include this activity in your regular journal or keep a special journal for this purpose.**

- **Make a conscious decision to be more grateful.** Do not merely write down lists of things to be grateful for, but carry your attitude of gratitude with you into your daily life. This will make your journaling more effective.

- **Write only one to two times per week.** Psychologist Sonja Lyubomirsky and her colleagues found in one study that people who wrote in their gratitude journals once a week for six weeks reported more happiness than people who wrote more often. This may be due to how quickly the mind becomes habituated to certain tasks, even pleasant ones.

- **Be detailed.** Elaborate on why you are grateful for someone or something. What do they add to your life? What would it be like not to have them available to you?

- **Focus on people.** People are more important than things in your gratitude practice. How have certain people changed your life? What are some of the important things you have learned from them? If you feel like it's appropriate, write a thank you note or make a gratitude call to express what they've meant to you in life.

 *Quiz: Take an Online Gratitude Quiz*

Take The Gratitude Quiz posted online by the Greater Good Science Center. The 20-item Quiz is based on a scale developed by psychologists Mitch Adler and Nancy Fagley.[3] Answers are submitted and scored with results online. http://greatergood.berkeley.edu/quizzes/take_quiz/6/

TOOL #3: BOOST YOUR RESILIENCE VIA MEDIA TOOLS

The following tools are easy to use and offer big dividends: greater confidence, a happier attitude, and skills for handling life's inevitable challenges.

1. Read and view uplifting stories and websites. Reduce your time watching upsetting world news. Instead, look at daily affirmations online, such as Louise Hay's affirmation site: **http://www.louisehay.com/affirmations/** Or go to the following *Huffington Post* site to find a list of 15 positive websites, such as "The Happiness Project" and "Zen Habits" to bookmark for a rainy day **http://www.huffingtonpost.com/amy-neumann/15-uplifting-sites-focuse_b_1297094.html** Along this line of positive "input," read uplifting and encouraging stories such as those collected in the *Chicken Soup* series.

> There are a multitude of media tools to help you to handle everything life can throw at you. If you feed yourself with a diet of positive input, you can build up your hardiness or stress-resistance in the face of any change and transition.

2. Search out stories of resilient people. Read books or watch documentaries or films about individuals who have shown resilience in the face of great odds. For example, watch the Ken Burns documentary *The Roosevelts: An Intimate History*, which is part of his American history series. http://www.pbs.org/kenburns/films/the-roosevelts

3. Begin to collect inspiring quotes to review when you need a lift. Write them down in a journal. Or choose a book such as *The Elbert Hubbard Scrapbook*. This book is a classic! It includes the words of the greats from history and literature--from William Shakespeare and Benjamin Franklin to Charlotte Bronte and Charles Dickens.

4. Help someone in need. Volunteering your time and attention to do something for someone else is a great way to put your own difficulties in perspective. Go to "Volunteer Match" or a similar online site to help find a cause of special interest to you: **https://www.volunteermatch.org/**

5. Use a mantra. This can be the slow and loving repetition of any uplifting word of your choice, such as love, gratitude, or peace. A powerful, non-denominational word to use is HU (pronounced in a long out-breath like the man's name, Hugh). This is an ancient name for God, one held sacred by ancient cultures and peoples from all over the world. Singing HU everyday uplifts, protects, centers, and brings the individual into contact with his or her spiritual source. Visit **http://youtu.be/86nEoiyNar8** to experience the five-minute HU sound as it is sung by a multitude of voices online.

6. Do something! Try to find one thing you can do to make you feel that you are not a victim of your situation and that you are not helpless. This can be a single, small, concrete step toward trying to improve your circumstances.

 *Activity: Choose One!*

The activity for this section is to choose and implement one new task from the suggestions listed above. (Give it 21 days to form a new habit!) Write about this experience and how adding this tool has changed your life in any way.

_____

_____

_____

_____

_____

_____

_____

_____

_____

_____

TOOL #4: BALANCE YOUR MASCULINE AND FEMININE QUALITIES

The Masculine-Feminine Continuum

Talking about the balance of masculine-feminine energies is not a reference to gender or sex roles but to ways of being, of relating to others, and of expressing ourselves. All of us, whether male or female, have within us both masculine and feminine energies. We utilize these energies in how we react and respond to events, how we give to and receive from others, and how we communicate in daily life.

There is a continuum of masculinity-femininity: people, regardless of sex, may move to different points along this sliding scale depending on innate personality, habitual behavior, environment, past experiences, and specific situations and persons they may meet up with at any one time. However, individuals tend to find their personal masculine-feminine equilibrium or comfort zone on this scale, and when they move away from this balance point for extended periods of time, they tend to feel out-of-kilter, exhausted, unhealthy, and dysfunctional.

> All of us possess masculine and feminine qualities to one degree or another. Each person has a unique way of expressing the qualities that make up the masculine-feminine continuum. The key for health and well-being is to be able to access the right quality at the right time and to apply it to the appropriate degree! The more balanced you are on the M-F Scale, the easier this is.

If you can easily access and apply both of these energies, then you have a wider range of possible responses to life than the person who is stuck in only one approach or at one end of the continuum. The trick is being able to apply a more masculine or feminine energy to a situation at the right time and to the correct degree. Finding your own inner balance on the masculine-feminine scale allows you to be more resilient in life and is an important step toward psychological wholeness and well-being.

A Matter of Opposites

Before we can talk about integrating and balancing masculine and feminine energies, however, we need to separate them to define them. Below are a few of the qualities associated with the masculine and feminine. (These energies are also known by the Taoistic terms Yin and Yang).

MASCULINE (Yang)	**FEMININE (Yin)**
logical, analytical	intuitive, insightful
assertive, active	receptive, passive
rational	emotional
independent, individualistic	interdependent, relational
strong	gentle
competitive	cooperative
extroversion	introversion
confident	modest
decisive	process-oriented
providing	nurturing
risk-taking	cautious
rough, tough	soft/gentle
freedom-seeking	restrictive
directed	unfocused
confident	insecure
intolerant	patient
external	internal
blunt	graceful
society and outwardly oriented	family and inwardly oriented

Extreme Qualities Become Shadow Qualities

It is important to remember that any quality taken to extreme becomes an unhealthy liability or a "shadow" quality. For example, when taken too far, the masculine quality of being dominant or a strong leader can become domination or tyranny, being uncompromising can become stubbornness or rigidity, and having conviction or commitment can turn into narrow-mindedness. The feminine quality of modesty can turn into low self-esteem, intuition can transform into ungroundedness and fuzzy thinking, connectedness can become loss of boundaries or a weak sense of self. This is why it's necessary to strengthen those qualities that are weak and to diminish those that tend to be over-emphasized.

Shadow qualities are unbalanced and extreme behaviors--and because our behavior is connected to our bodily health--we can suffer physically from these imbalances. The left hemisphere of your brain represents the logical, concrete, analytical masculine side of your brain and the right side of your body; the right hemisphere of your brain controls the emotional, creative, and intuitive side of your brain and the left side of your body. The side of your body that has aches and pains will give you a clue about what is out-of-kilter in your behavior. Many physical diseases and ailments can be associated with imbalances, such as overly driven and stress-inducing behaviors leading to heart attacks and strokes or fertility issues.

Balance Brings Health and Wholeness

Masculine and feminine qualities are equally valuable! To be truly resilient through change and transition, you need to be able to call on both sets of qualities, as some situations require you to be more masculine—assertive, action-oriented, and outgoing--and others call on you to be more feminine—receptive, nurturing, and reflective. Combining and integrating these energies allow you greater mental and physical health, including increased personal authority, strengthened boundaries, greater freedom from compulsive behaviors, and more stability in the face of change and transition.

Journaling: Where On The Continuum?

Review each job description below and mark on the Masculine-Feminine Continuum where you think the individual who does this job would be positioned. Then, do the same for yourself and answer questions relating to you and your life.

1. Job Descriptions: Where would the individuals who perform each of the following jobs be likely to fall on the M-F Scale below? Persons who are attracted to certain jobs tend to have the qualities required for the performance of that job.

M_____F

With an "X" mark, indicate on the Masculine-Feminine Scale where you would put someone who is hired as Project Manager for a manufacturing company. Project managers determine timelines, resources and budgets for multiple projects in plants and factories. In addition, project managers lead, coach and motivate other workers on projects and write project status reports for upper management.

M_____F

With an "X" mark, indicate on the Masculine-Feminine Scale where you would put someone who is an Air Traffic Controller. Controllers maintain radio and radar contact with aircraft pilots within delineated areas, providing them with instructions and information about weather conditions and safe flight, as well as ascent and descent paths.

M_____F

With an "X" mark, indicate on the Masculine-Feminine Scale where you would put someone who works as an Art Therapist. An art therapist helps patients resolve their emotional and mental difficulties via the artistic process. Some of the art forms through which the art therapist might help patients express themselves are painting, sculpting, theater, or dance.

M_____F

With an "X" mark, indicate on the Masculine-Feminine Scale where you would put someone who works as a secondary school teacher. Secondary school teachers educate children between the ages of 11 and 18 in a subject area based on a state curriculum. Typical responsibilities include spending class time with students, preparing lesson plans, checking and evaluating work, arranging parent conferences, attending staff meetings, monitoring extracurricular activities, and participating in ongoing professional development.

M_____F

2. Where do you think you are positioned on the above masculine-feminine continuum? Mark your own position with an "X". How do your qualities, as reflected by this place on the scale, affect your relationships, your job, recreational activities, or any other part of your life?

_____

_____

_____

_____

_____

_____

_____

3. What specific things can you do to become more balanced in your behaviors and in your way of relating and responding to events and to others?

Remember that everyone has their own masculine-feminine balance point! To check whether you are in or out of alignment with your own balance point, ask yourself, "How well is my life going?" For example, it may be appropriate to be decisive, focused, directive and assertive at work, but if you are bringing CEO behaviors home with you, your intimate relationships may suffer. Or perhaps there is a decided lack of assertiveness and self-confidence in the workplace and this carries over to a passivity and inactivity at home, leading to an apparent inability to accomplish work-related goals as well as to demonstrate commitment in relationships. Too much or too little expression of both sets of qualities seem to bring unhappiness and dissatisfaction in life.

_____
_____
_____
_____
_____
_____
_____

Inventory: The BEM Sex Role Inventory (BSRI)

Take the BEM Sex Role Inventory, developed in 1971 by Dr. Sandra Bem. The Inventory, which is based on gender stereotypes, characterizes your personality as masculine, feminine, androgynous, or undifferentiated. The Inventory measures how well you fit into traditional sex roles. Of course, a lot has changed since 1971, so your score may reflect changes in cultural expectations as well as information about your approach to life. **http://garote.bdmonkeys.net/bsri.html**

In The Next Chapter
There are times when something happens in our lives--the death of someone we love dearly, the collapse of our financial foundation, the onset of a devastating illness or disability--that triggers a process that pulls us into a long, drawn-out cycle of disillusionment, doubt, and despair. This extended period of turmoil is sometimes called the *Dark Night of Soul*. During this time, everything by which you once defined yourself falls away; you may begin this process by asking "Why me?" and finally, progress to questioning the meaning of life and your purpose in it. In **Chapter Five**, this transformative experience is explored. We will consider what this process looks and feels like, how to collaborate with it, and what we can learn from it.

CHAPTER FIVE:
The Dark Night of Soul

Some changes look negative on the surface but you will soon realize that space is being created in your life for something new to emerge.

~Eckhart Tolle

All changes, even the most longed for, have their melancholy; for what we leave behind us is a part of ourselves; we must die to one life before we can enter another.

~Anatole France

Post-Traumatic Growth: Bouncing Forward

The tumult and trouble of a major life crisis or transition can leave a lot of personal change in its wake. Fortunately, the change and transition process can be worked with in such a way that positive psychological transformation, or *post-traumatic growth*, is possible as the end-result or outcome. Instead of highlighting the effects of post-traumatic stress, the following chapter will focus on the post-traumatic growth that can occur through the struggle with a traumatic event.

> In the past, resilience has often been about surviving difficult times rather than becoming a victim of them. Today, research on Post-Traumatic Growth is exploring how people can not only survive but how they can grow through adversity!

It is possible for challenging life experiences to produce many beneficial personal changes. One of these changes has to do with *self-perception*. People who allow themselves to be transformed through trauma and crisis report more self-confidence, increased self-reliance and greater competence in dealing with difficult situations. Another important change that often occurs is in *relationships to others*. After a traumatic event, people often re-establish lost relationships and strengthen their social support by accepting help from others. Finally, deep-seated change often brings about a revised *philosophy of life*, including a more positive outlook, reorganization of life's priorities, greater appreciation for the gift of life, and a stronger spiritual and religious orientation.

Golden Nuggets of Meaning

Below are several examples of people who have gone beyond survivorship because they have not only bounced back from hardship but have bounced *forward*. In each of these examples, individuals faced situations that would be supremely challenging for any one of us; yet, they managed to dig out the golden nuggets of meaning from their experiences. The post-traumatic growth reported by these persons include greater awareness, renewed spiritual connection, and a mission to give back to life in some way.

> It's evident from reading the vignettes in this section that what happens to someone is not as important as the perception of the event's meaning. Believing that everything has a purpose is an essential characteristic of persons who develop resiliency and experience personal growth through adversity.

In her TED talk, Stacey Kramer claims that her brain tumor turned out to be "the best thing that ever happened to me." She says her tumor brought many benefits into her life, such as reconnecting with family and friends, finding new meaning in life, reprioritizing what was important to her, achieving a new understanding and appreciation of her body, and redefining her spiritual foundation.

In 2009, after an MRI to examine the cause of a twitching eye, Tom O'Donnell was told that he had a cancerous brain tumor. Only 45 years old, he underwent surgery that removed 60 percent of the tumor, or *oligodendroglioma* (Tom has pointed out that the term has the word "god" embedded in it). When he awoke from surgery and was still able to physically function, he decided to take up long-distance running. Since that time, he has run ten marathons, primarily to raise money for brain tumor research. Tom states, "Everything happens for a reason. I thank God every day for allowing me to share my experiences with others and in some small way offer hope…My journey continues. However, my plan is to live the rest of my life."

In a blog for the *Huffington Post*, Heather Martin related the trauma of losing two business partnerships in just one year. After filing for bankruptcy and cashing out her retirement funds, she was desolate. Heather points out, however, that "Adversity is one of the greatest blessings of our life if we seize the moment to dig deeper and evolve." Her financial hard times actually left her better off: she is now more willing to take calculated risks, has a better perspective on so-called failures, and is able to "find emotional stability, spiritual peace, and a deep understanding of what life means…"

The Dark Night of Soul

In **Chapter Two**, we learned that the two most important qualities you need to meet life with a resilient attitude are *flexibility* and *persistence*. But what if, beyond flexibility and single-minded persistence, a life crisis requires a long period of profound psychological

> Sometimes a traumatic event triggers a long, drawn-out period of emotional and psychological upheaval. A process of inner transformation and healing begins that cannot be controlled but only collaborated with; this process is essentially a spiritual journey. It's important to emphasize that the dark night of soul isn't so much about crisis and catastrophe as it is about how people assimilate and integrate these experiences to become more self-aware and spiritually connected.

re-orientation and inner change? This protracted process, which may necessitate fewer work hours, decreased social activity, and psychotherapeutic support, is so difficult some call it the *dark night of soul*. Briefly, we will look at what the dark night looks and feels like, what its purpose is, how to successfully navigate it, and what is gained from this process.

Sometimes the event that triggers this process--a difficult divorce, the death of a loved one, a diagnosis of a catastrophic illness--is so traumatic that individuals' lives are turned upside down. People may even lose everything in life that they once identified with--job, house, money, titles, perhaps spouse and family. As they are brought to the very edge, they may wonder who they truly are.

Strange Symptoms

During the dark night period, people may feel lethargic, anxious, and sad. Their frantic attempts to fix things--with increased activity, a new spouse, alcohol or some other type of self-medication--do not work. They may need to confront unresolved conflicts from childhood, which often come up for review during these tumultuous times. Deep depression, mental paralysis, and physical exhaustion can bring panic and confusion. They may experience doubts, fears, desolation, and rage. They may also suffer vague aches and pains, develop strange eating habits and their senses--such as hearing and smelling--sometimes become excruciatingly sensitive. In some cases, people may have unusually tumultuous dreams, full of devastating storms, earthquakes, and other disasters.

> **Psychological turmoil and related symptoms during the dark night of soul are sometimes made more difficult by well-meaning friends and relatives who want you to simply "snap out of it," or "pull yourself up by the bootstraps." They have not been educated to know about this process, and so do not understand that it is an organic, natural process of transformative change that for many, leads to greater spiritual awareness.**

If prior to the dark night experience, individuals have had had normally stable lives, chances are this process is meant to wake them to the deeper meaning and purpose of life. The dark night is an opportunity to reprioritize what's truly important in life and to ask fundamental questions, such as: *What is my purpose for being here? What is missing in my life? Who and what am I giving my energy and attention to? Am I being spiritually guided?*

Triggering Events

The following vignette illustrates how a woman was triggered by a confluence of events to seek support and clarity through a psychotherapeutic process that, as it unfolded, became an extended dark night journey.

> Sue had suffered a "perfect storm of losses": her efforts to start her own yoga studio had failed, and she was now broke, exhausted, angry, confused, and disillusioned. Sue had made a great "leap of faith" to realize her dream, pouring everything she had--time, money, prospects--into her studio. When her business failed to launch, Sue felt that she had lost her vision as well as her sense of self. To survive, she took a job that served survival needs but left her feeling uninspired and depressed. During this time, Sue's mother unexpectedly died, and Sue was completely devastated with grief--and an even greater sense of loss.
>
> As we began our work together, it was apparent that Sue remembered remarkably little about her childhood. In fact, she seemed to suffer from amnesia, a nearly total memory loss that extended from early childhood through her high school and early college years. When she looked at childhood photos of herself, Sue could barely recognize the little girl in the picture because she had repressed so much of her early life.
>
> Sue began the hard work of uncovering and reclaiming her childhood. She spent time looking through family photo albums and calling childhood friends and relatives to ask questions about her family. Before passing, Sue's mother had bequeathed her personal journals to Sue and her brother. These journals, 60 in all, chronicled daily family life over several decades and were an extraordinary and timely treasure trove for Sue. Carefully poring over the notebooks, Sue was shocked at all she had forgotten, including the details surrounding the death of a close middle school friend.

When there is no organic cause, wholesale repression of a complete childhood history is nearly always an indication that something traumatic has occurred at a young age. Because children do not have the intellectual maturity or ego strength to deal with an early traumatic event, the incident is often repressed. In the fullness of time, relevant early childhood information often surfaces naturally via dreams, memories, and exploratory therapy sessions.

With the help of Sue's family-related research, intermittent bodywork, her conscientious recording of her dreams, and her attention to daily synchronicities--or the "waking dream"--we were gradually able to piece together her childhood. The "hard truths" of family fights, alcoholism, and other hallmarks of dysfunction in her mother's journals painted a very different picture for Sue from what she had fantasized her childhood to be. Her dreams, becoming more specific over time, began making references to a loved and trusted male relative molesting her when she was a little girl. Shocked to her core, Sue could not reconcile this idea with the man she had once adored. In one relevant dream, a man had come into her home and stolen her computer; this was an apt analogy for the "wiping out" of her memories by her relative's damaging actions. An insistent stream of synchronicities supported this information: in her day-to-day life, Sue continuously saw a series of unusual items that she specifically associated with this particular relative and repeatedly encountered meaningful book titles which clearly spoke to her of the truth.

Sue was slowly able to acknowledge, process, and assimilate the shattering incidents that had hijacked her childhood. Achieving this level of acceptance required that she first experience a dark night of soul, a long drawn-out process of suffering, confusion, loss, disorientation, and vulnerability. Everything that Sue had ever believed about herself and her family had been smashed; having "touched the bottom of her own well" of sorrow, she began to rebuild.

Sue initially experienced the loss of her professional dreams, her income, her self-confidence, and her trust in life. Then she lost her mother, and finally, her most cherished ideas regarding her early home life and the people she had loved and trusted. But she gained a great deal, too. Sue's transformational journey was primarily fueled by the uncovering of childhood violations; dealing with this issue ultimately enabled her to become more grounded, "to see things as they are," and to become more accepting of herself and others.

What Can You Do?

The dark night of soul process forces you to *slow down*. You may need to take a leave from work to somehow retreat from life's routines for a while. This is a time to reflect, to reevaluate your life, and to align yourself with your spiritual center. This is a time to enjoy the feminine principle which encourages *be-ing* rather than *do-ing* (or *hav-ing!*) Reducing time on the computer and cell or in watching television is helpful during this phase of the dark night. Cutting back on distractions and social engagements is also supportive of this process.

As described in **Chapter One** when discussing the middle stage, or Neutral Zone of a transition, there are certain activities that you can do. These activities allow you to collaborate with a process that cannot be directed by an act of will. Some of these activities bear repeating: gardening, sculpting or painting, playing with pets, walking in a park or near the ocean or a lake, journaling, working with your dreams, reading and writing poetry, listening to music created by the world's great composers, or, if you are able, playing a musical instrument yourself, making soups and nourishing meals for yourself, participating in yoga or other mind-body-spirit physical exercises, and reading uplifting, spiritually-oriented literature. Maintaining an attitude of reverence and gratitude (even though you may not fully understand what is happening to you) is also important during this time.

> A less aggressive, more receptive attitude is called for during the dark night process. When life as you have known it comes to an end, you must wait for the natural cycle of things to change (another way to put this is learning "to wait on the hand of God"). Fortunately, there are things you can do during this time of waiting that will help you cultivate a positive, interactive relationship with your process.

Who Gets Through the Dark Night of Soul?

If you consent to see your process to its natural end—and not short-circuit it out of fear or impatience—your life will open up again in new and fruitful ways. Persons who have successfully navigated the dark night are usually characterized by the following:

- They have strong spiritual aspirations and some background in spiritual studies or in techniques/disciplines such as meditation and prayer.

- They have stable social support structures.

- They are able to find sources of counsel or guidance, such as from members of the clergy or from mental health professionals.

- They have the capacity for insight and change.

- They can tolerate a lack of clarity and a period of confusion.
- They do not have a history of mental illness and can clearly distinguish consensual reality from fantasy.

- Previous to their dark night experience, they have maintained stable jobs and relationships and have demonstrated a functional, healthy attitude toward life.

What Is the Purpose of the Dark Night?

The enemy of self-awareness is complacency. The dark night experience shakes us by the shoulders and reminds us that we are destined for far more than being preoccupied with mere everyday existence: we are *stopped in our tracks* and taken out of conventional life by the dark night process so that we can realize there is a greater spiritual reality and we are part of it. This experience helps us to learn the limits of the individual will and personal resources; when we *hit a wall* we learn to surrender our will and the situation we're in to something "higher." The dark night process is a way to resolve childhood wounds, to clear dysfunctional patterns, to experience immediate and real contact with spiritual energies, and to learn that we are much more than the ego-self. The dark night of soul is an aspect of a spiritual unfoldment process of psychological and spiritual transformation that is embedded in the genetic blueprint of every human being.

> The dark night takes us below the surface of life. The dark night can show us the healing power of the feminine principle (think of the Chinese description of "yin") in its appreciation of the cycles of time and nature. The feminine principle is also at work in the process of human transformation and regeneration: we learn during the dark night that we do not have to physically die to experience psychological death and rebirth.

What Are the Benefits?

As the end of the dark night experience, life seems to begin again. We are finally "spit up on dry land" and new opportunities offer themselves. We unexpectedly get a call about a new job or we meet a person who interests us as a possible new relationship. Life goes on, but we have changed.

There are certain ways that a dark night of soul benefits those who have successfully navigated this process: the veterans of the dark night experience have learned more about themselves, they have reconnected to their spiritual Source, and they have discovered a desire to give back to their communities in some way. Such persons have gone from "me" to "we."

Other benefits acquired through the dark night process include the realization of greater material detachment, the healing of childhood wounds and conflicts, the release of guilt, the forgiveness of self and others, and the reconsideration of what's truly important in life. Persons often become more inner-directed and less concerned with what others think. Personal qualities such as compassion, honesty, trust, compassion, humility, and a service-orientation have been enhanced through the tests and trials of the dark night of soul.

> Humans seem to grow the most through conflict, hardship, and adversity. The difficulties of the dark night are akin to a great tempering through the fires of suffering. But this is suffering that helps people to purify the little self so that a spiritual connection can be made to the Higher Self, or to the immortal part of ourselves.

More Information on the Dark Night of Soul

If you would like to know more about the dark night of soul, you can read my book, *Drinking the Dragon: Stories of the Dark Night of Soul* as well as do the exercises in the interactive companion workbook, *Drinking the Dragon: Process Workbook*. (go to my website to purchase: **www.TransitionTherapist.com**). For the book, I interviewed several people who had faced the death of a spouse or a child, had survived childhood abuse, had overcome serious illness, and had been confronted with other traumatic life events. They each describe the stormy weather of their dark nights but also the ultimate triumphs at the end of their tribulations. You can also take the *Dark Night of Soul Inventory* in the Appendices of *Navigating Change* for greater insight into your current situation.

 ## Quiz: Take a Post-Traumatic Growth Questionnaire!

Go online at **http://www.drrahe.com/detail/223/** to take a *Post-Traumatic Growth Questionnaire*. The 25-item questionnaire will take about 15 minutes to complete and self-score. It is recommended that this inventory be taken after some time has passed after experiencing a profound crisis or difficulty. It may take time for you to see change in the areas assessed by this questionnaire: appreciation of life, relating to others, new possibilities, personal strength, and spiritual change. Most people show more growth in some areas than in others, and many show growth in different areas at different times. If your results concern you, you are encouraged to seek out professional health and mental health care.

What was your Questionnaire personal score and percentage?
Score_____ Percentage_____

Discuss your Questionnaire results on the lines below:

Journaling: Character Strengths

It's important to know what strengths you can count on when the times get tough—and which strengths you need to cultivate. Do the following activity to assess how prepared you are to face your next challenge!

I HAVE: what external supports to you have in your life? These supports would include family, a circle of friends, church affiliation, business colleagues, etc. Write your own list on the lines below:

_____
_____
_____
_____
_____
_____
_____

I AM: this is a list of the internal strengths you already possess. Such a list might include a person with a strong spiritual center, someone with a healthy sense of optimism, or an individual known for having a caring nature.

_____
_____
_____
_____

I CAN: this category includes interpersonal and problem-solving skills that you already have: you may have strong communication skills, good problem-solving abilities, or you are excellent at very quickly sizing up people and situations.

_____

_____

_____

_____

I WILL: list the supports, strengths, or skills that you wish to build up or enhance to be better prepared for difficulties. For example, you may want to spend more time cultivating an inner life by journaling or working with your dreams.

_____

_____

_____

_____

_____

_____

_____

In The Next Chapter
How does culture change? If a culture is made up of an aggregate of individuals, then when we change the culture must, too! This brings to mind Mahatma Gandhi's famous statement, "Be the change you want to see in the world." When we undergo deep-seated transformation by a process such as the dark night of soul, we are unconsciously affecting change in our communities, culture and even the world-at-large.

CHAPTER SIX:
Individual Transformation and Cultural Change

I change the world, the world changes me.

~Libba Bray

The world changes in direct proportion to the number of people willing to be honest about their lives.

~Armistead Maupin

What we achieve inwardly will change outer reality.

~Plutarch

Take Charge of Change

The difference between swimming and drowning in a sea of change has everything to do with how prepared you are to meet voluntary, and especially involuntary, changes. An example of an involuntary change is when the business that employs you suddenly downsizes or goes bankrupt, and you are forced to look for new work. A voluntary change is when you decide to become trained to move into a different department at your corporation, as you see certain market trends are occurring and you want to be in a position to work in another capacity either at your current site of employment or elsewhere.

Regardless of whether it's voluntary or involuntary, you can expect to change jobs today many times during your life span. According to the *Bureau of Labor Statistics,* the average worked today stays at his or her job for 4.4 years and Millennials (born between 1977-1997) stay at their jobs for fewer than three years! Regardless of the type of work you do, you can look for upcoming trends and prepare to take advantage of future opportunities. Here are a few suggestions:

- Look for trends by reading magazines (some, like *Futurist Magazine,* specialize in trends), watching television, talking to people, browsing websites.

- Join a professional organization or a union to get information on upcoming changes in your particular area of work.

- Decide to act in response to these trends: read a book, take a training, go back to school, or become an apprentice to someone in order to prepare for work changes and future opportunities.

Responding to Trends: Stephen's Story

How can you prepare yourself for change that initially, seems forced upon you? The following vignette illustrates how an individual responded to an involuntary change at work.

> When Stephen was 49 years old, he was laid off as a printing press technician when new equipment was purchased by the print company owners. Instead of being upset, Stephen was actually relieved. He had been catching unsettling rumors here and there and had been living in uncertainty about his job for some

time. Now he could move forward. As an avid user of technology, Stephen was fascinated by computer-generated imagery, or CGI. He utilized his unemployment time to research training programs in 3D computer graphics. He also looked for companies using CGI applications in video games, commercials, films, and television programs. Stephen was both anxious and excited about beginning a new career. He looked forward to finding work in the field of his dreams.

Because Stephen expected change and had been reading about upcoming trends and prospects in the field of his interest, he was in a good position to take action. Stephen turned what could have been an unfortunate situation into a new and exciting opportunity.

 ## *Journaling: What Changes Do You Foresee?*

The job front represents only one area of societal change. Reflect on the changes you think may occur in the following life areas in the coming years. For example, what forms do you think family life will take by 2030?

1. Family life:
___
___
___
___
___
___

2. Your current occupation:
___
___
___
___
___
___

3. Education:

_____
_____
_____
_____
_____

4. Life styles: Living arrangements:

_____
_____
_____
_____
_____

5. Entertainment:

_____
_____
_____
_____
_____

6. Religion:

_____
_____
_____
_____
_____

Possible Trends of the Future

What will the future look like? Though no one can say for sure, it's helpful to look at a few societal trends as well as innovations in medicine, life-style, education, religion, and warfare. Emerging technologies and developments give us some idea of potential changes across the U.S. as well as around the world. These possible occurrences have been culled from journals, institutes, and think-tank experts:

> From HIV-testing and Smartphone devices to human colonization expeditions (the Mars One Settlement) and futuristic concrete modular abodes, change is ever constant in our lives. New trends can make our lives more stressful as well as more interesting and diversified!

Demographic Change

Changes in the number of humans on this planet is one of the most impactful factors in creating wide-ranging change in the next two decades or so:

- Globally, the population by 2030 is expected to reach 8.3 billion, resulting in possible food, water and energy shortages. On a brighter note, leading experts from around the world are offering solutions, including recycling wastewater, using energy-efficient desalination in plants, promoting international cooperation to address water pollution, preparing insects, algae and seaweed for greater consumption, and spending less money on defense and more on food production.

- In the U.S., the most significant change is the aging population. By 2030, there will be about 72.1 million older persons. In fact, people 65 and over are expected to grow to be 19% of the population by 2030. Another demographic trend is the rise in single-person households, caused by loss of a spouse, divorce, and persons getting married late in life or not at all. (Currently, 42 percent of the U.S. population is unmarried). Older parents, one-parent families, and less traditional family constellations are related trends.

Fourth-Wave Feminism

The push for gender equality is increasing world-wide in the areas of politics, corporate leadership, media, education and religion. Beyond feminism, the *feminine principle* is coming to the fore, especially in western society. This principle, which is expressed through both men and women, brings with it a growing appreciation of the values of cooperation, connection, collaboration, community, and communication over those of competition, hierarchy, conflict, self-interest, and domination. Environmental concerns, peace-making efforts, and social responsibility as well as personal growth and development are also within the realm of the feminine principle. The values of the feminine principle lead the way to the change that is necessary to a better world.

Happiness and Authenticity

Materialism may be losing its allure. People are working harder and longer to earn more, but studies show that once earned income goes beyond $75,000, money does not significantly impact the level of happiness. According to *Future Files*, a book filled with forecasts about how the world might change in the next half century, we are suffering from Too Much Information (TMI), Too Many Choices (TMC), and Too Much Technology (TMT). Consequently, people are seeking greater fulfillment and authenticity.

Spirituality

A 2012 summary of the results from a Pew Research Center's Forum on Religion & Public Life, conducted in tandem with the PBS television program *Religion & Ethics NewsWeekly*, shows that one-fifth of the U.S. public—and a third of adults who are under 30 years old—are religiously unaffiliated today. This number includes 13 million atheists and agnostics, with an additional 33 million (sometimes called "nones") reporting no particular religious affiliation at all. An interesting finding of the survey is that many in the "nones" group are religious or spiritual in at least some way.

What does this sub-group of "nones" believe?

- two-thirds (68%) of the unaffiliated claim they believe in God
- more than half (58%) feel a deep connection to nature and the earth
- more than third (37%) classify themselves as "spiritual" but not religious
- one-in-five (21%) say they pray every day

The growth of the "nones" is largely due to generational replacement, or the gradual replacement of older generations with newer ones. While the summary reports that many "nones" think that traditional religion is too concerned with power, politics, and money, it will be of interest in the next decades to see if there is a movement toward new forms of spiritual expression within this sub-group of religiously unaffiliated.

Climate Change

The Environmental Protection Agency (EPA) projects that, depending on the level of future greenhouse gas emissions and natural influences such as volcanic activity and changes in the sun's intensity, the global average temperature by 2100 is expected to warm at least twice as much as it has during the last 100 years. The National Intelligence Council forecasts that the severity of weather patterns will worsen, with wet areas getting wetter, and dry areas becoming more arid. Largely due to melting ice cover, global sea levels have risen 8 inches in the last 130 years and are projected to rise 2.5' to 6.5' by 2100. All this means is that we will need to modify our lifestyles in an attempt to lessen the severity of these changes as well as to adapt to such changes as they occur.

Robotics

A new era of robotics may be on its way. Robots will be increasingly used in assembly lines, elder care and nursing assistance, in education, militarization, and home maintenance. Machines with human-level intelligence may be achieved in another 50-75 years. A few innovative uses for robotics, some of which are already in place, are given below:

- Soldiers will soon wear protective and strength-enhancing iron suits that work via remote control. DARPA has developed "Spot," a stealth military robot that carries gear for soldiers, follows a unit over rough terrain, and obeys simple visual and auditory commands.

- Robot companions are also being engineered, such as Mobiserv. This robot tells a convalescing senior, for example, when to take medicine or to go on walks and other health-related reminders. Senior citizens may also enjoy greater mobility wearing exoskeletons, which provide muscular strength and support.
- Small, close-to-the-ground robots are taking never-before-seen videos of animals living in their natural habitats in the Serengeti.

- There are even robotic systems that can ice the perfect birthday cake!

Medicine

The field of medicine and healthcare is one of the fastest-growing areas of innovative ideas and developments. Below are just a few promising technological advances in this field:

- Gene therapy and longevity research will be emphasized in the coming two decades.

- Medical uses of wearable health technology, which is already widely used in sports and fitness, now includes everything from headsets that measure brainwave activity to clothing that features built-in sensors. Wearable medical devices that measure glucose, blood pressure and heart rate monitors will become common.

- A new mental health classification may appear for gamers who engage in long-term virtual sessions interacting with violent war games: virtual post-traumatic stress disorder (vPTSD).

- Holographic keyboards will project medical data on walls and tabletops.

- DNA analysis will be at the patient's bedside and will help to accurately prescribe drugs for the patient's individualized genome.

The Work Force

Futurist Magazine innovation editor Thomas Frey reports that two billion jobs will disappear by 2030. However, replacement jobs are currently being invented. In addition, tomorrow's workers will develop a variety of skills that will allow them to find out what other people need doing and then accomplishing it. Frey's list of job-inventing industries include 3-D printing, biofactories, personal rapid transit systems, innovative living and learning environments, and more. By 2020, three-fourths of U.S. jobs will likely require higher skills for higher pay, challenging the shrinking labor pool to get further training to meet these needs.

Black Swan Events

Cultural and world trends can be greatly impacted by the unexpected and out-of-the-ordinary. *Black Swan*[4] shocks are random and unforeseen events that have major effects on human life. Such events are extremely difficult to predict: they can include a severe pandemic, overwhelming climate change, economic collapse, nuclear, chemical or biological weapon attack, large-scale cyber-assault, solar geomagnetic storms that knock out electrical grids, and other major and unexpected occurrences. However, black swans are not always negative. Examples of positive black swans would be the invention of the Internet or the Harry Potter phenomenon. Sometimes black swans influence people to make great personal changes and force them to take creative risks which result in progress for all humankind.

New Expressions of Life Experience

In addition to the previous forecast of innovations and ideas, a few areas of living experience that are transitioning to new expressions and manifestations are identified in the chart below:

CONDITIONS OF THE PAST IN TRANSITION

Identification with roles or man or woman	Integration and application of both masculine and feminine energy patterns within each individual; home and work roles cease to be divided into sex-appropriate categories
"Completing one another" in a symbiotic relationship; dependency on other person to supply intellectual or emotional traits in lieu of developing these in oneself	Coming together in relationship as two persons working toward individual wholeness; assisting each other toward Self-Realization and in the completion of spiritual assignments/missions
Religious/spiritual intermediaries, including New Age "mini-gurus," mediums, channelers, etc.	Personal spiritual experiences with the Higher Self, the "voice" within, or w/Spirit as the Light and Sound
Non-conventional spiritual experiences largely seen as pathological	These experiences understood as possibly initiatory. Spiritually trained practitioners assist people having emergent spiritual experiences

Projection of "all that is bad" onto others	Taking personal responsibility for negative traits and behaviors
Belief that we are alone in the universe	Realization of galactic citizenship
Competition, "winning" at all costs, adversarial relationships	Cooperation, collaboration, community, connection, collective efforts
"Me" values: self-serving, greedy	"We" values: service above self, shared wealth
Toxic Food: GMOs, hormones, sprays, additives, sugars, etc.	"Back to earth" and green movements, people growing their own vegetables, more community gardens. Insistence on eating only food that has not been altered or tampered with.
Psychotropic and/or perscription drugs for all that ails	More preventative, holistic approaches emphasized: Reiki, acupuncture, color and sound healing, etc.
Classroom education that is book/computer and test-oriented. Teachers as educational authorities and dispensers.	Back to education systems that offer on-the-job vocational and skills training. Return to educational methods such as individualized learning contracts, creative "real-world" problem-solving, etc. Teachers as educational managers and guides
Fossil fuels	Alternative, non-environmental impact energy sources

Strategic Social Change

Unexpected social change can be driven by cultural, religious, economic, scientific or technological forces. But the Sustainable Development Goals (SDGs) set up for 2016-2030 by the United Nations[5] are focusing on how social change can be strategically planned to achieve specific objectives, such as:

- end poverty and hunger worldwide
- achieve gender equality and empowerment
- increase clean water availability
- provide affordable and reliable energy for all
- promote economic growth with productive employment and decent work for all
- ensure inclusive and equitable quality education for all
- take urgent action to combat climate change
- protect and restore terrestrial ecosystems (such as the oceans and rain forests) and prevent further biodiversity loss (animals and plants currently going extinct at an alarming rate)
- work together internationally to create more equality between countries, with the formation of economic global partnerships and institutions that promote justice for all

Human beings seem to work best when they are *at the edge of a cliff,* so perhaps in the next 15 to 20 years we will see remarkable preventative and remedial measures taken to solve many of our problems. But solving outer difficulties is only half of the challenge: we must also change *ourselves!*

An Interactive Relationship

We know that outer events create change in our lives, sometimes forcing us to make many accommodations. But how does personal inner change, especially the kind fueled by demanding processes like the dark night of soul, influence the changes we see around us in the culture and the world? In actuality, the individual mirrors society and society reflects the individual. There is an interactive, reciprocal relationship between people and the society in which they live.

> After the successful navigation of a dark night of soul experience, people find that they have transformed in significant ways. They report more self-awareness, a deeper connection to their spiritual center, and a desire to give back to their communities. It's a paradox that as persons become more uniquely themselves, they feel a more profound interconnection to humanity as a whole.

The personal dark night tribulations discussed in the previous chapter are the same upheavals we see in the wider culture: economic downturns, political turmoil, threats of terrorism, unexpected wide-scale disasters. Systems and institutions must fall apart to make way for their re-creation on a more functional, humanitarian level. The primary challenge is for humans to utilize the often chaotic "in between times," the period between old and new societal structures, to nurture and achieve new levels of consciousness that promote positive global change. Permanent, positive change can only take root in society when this type of deep-seated change occurs in the individuals who make up that society.

Shadow Work

A key to profound inner change is to do our shadow work. (The shadow was briefly described in **Chapter Three**). During the dark night process we "confront our shadow" at some point. What does this mean? We may get a dream in which we are running around saying very bad things about certain people, including a few friends. When we think about the dream and we are honest with ourselves, we realize that we really do enjoy spreading gossip a little too much. The dream is showing us a "shadow" part of ourselves, an aspect of ourselves that, until we had the dream, had been "hiding in the dark corners," below our conscious awareness. Another way to become aware of the unconscious things we say and do is to think of someone who really pushes our buttons, and to isolate just what trait in them irritates us so much. Chances are we have this very same trait and that we are projecting this unpleasantness onto someone else.

Facing the shadow, or our own negativity, is to take stock of ourselves--not to make us feel badly about ourselves, but to help us take responsibility for the damage we do when we remain unconscious of our faults. The task of "cleaning up our own back yards" helps us to make a true difference in the world. Recognizing and diminishing our own shadow allow us to become more stable, more whole, to have more personal authority and authenticity, to achieve better personal boundaries, and to become more creative.

Interestingly, entire nations can have a shadow, and they usually project this shadow onto other nations. The influx of intense spiritual energies, meant to raise general human awareness at this time of global change and transition, intensifies both positive and negative behavior: violence and conflict as well as positivity and peacefulness are strengthened and exaggerated. The world seems chaotic because old forms and institutions are falling apart and new ones haven't yet formed. It's more important than ever to know how to negotiate change and transition, as life seems to be speeding up with no signs of decelerating.

Map of Change

How you handle change in your life is important for yourself, for your family and the people who are close to you, to your community, to your culture—even for the world-at-large! It all comes down to you: how are you going to meet the next big challenge in your life?

In review, do the "Mapping Your Steps to Change" exercise below. The stages of change follow a definite pattern. The following exercise is a map of change. Work with this map to make your life change much easier, less bewildering, and more fulfilling. It may be helpful, too, to analyze a recent turning point using this map.[6]

EXERCISE

Mapping Your Steps to Change

_____
_____
_____

1. Write here about the change you are facing:
_____
_____
_____

2. Discover what inner obstacles--emotional and mental blocks--need to be removed for you to successfully navigate your change. Write about them on the lines below:
_____
_____
_____

3. Evaluate your current skills and then figure out how to get where you want to go:
_____
_____
_____

4. Once the change has taken place, what would this change you envision be like?
_____
_____
_____

5. Set a goal:
_____
_____
_____

6. Take one step toward that goal:
_____
_____
_____

7. What skills do you need to live in the new change?
_____
_____
_____

The Final Step

It's important to remember that when we do all we can do, we must ultimately hand over the change to God (or to whomever or whatever we conceive of as our Source). This is surrendering out of strength, not out of weakness. When we know that:

- life has a purpose
- we grow through change
- handling change well is the key to enjoying feelings of empowerment and freedom
- we grow in wisdom, understanding and compassion when we thoroughly process a change in our lives

then we are a long way on the path to learning and growing through change and transition.

Navigating Change: How to Go from Trauma to Transformation

ACKNOWLEDGMENTS

I want to thank all of the people in my life who have helped me through many difficult changes and transitions. There are persons, some of whom have passed and others who are still living, who have been extraordinarily kind, supportive, and influential during some very trying times. These individuals include relatives, friends, educators, psychotherapists, and spiritual teachers.

The challenging events in my life have generated many lessons, forced me into greater awareness, and increased my compassion for others. For two years in early adulthood I underwent a great transformational process, during which my ego structure, or "little self," was completely reformed and a connection was made to my Higher Self, or Soul. This experience has provided the platform for every interest and activity that I have been involved in since. Out of this process has come the understanding that my purpose is to help others become aware of their purpose.

This book is dedicated to that mission, as I hope that the message in its pages-- that change and transition bring growth--is supportive of people as they go about their daily lives and realize their individual life missions. *Navigating Change* was written with the idea that when people appreciate their true beauty and value as Soul, they will be able to live their lives with greater dexterity, love, and freedom.

Navigating Change: How to Go from Trauma to Transformation

FOOTNOTES

CHAPTER 2
1. These items were paraphrased from the more comprehensive WebMD quiz: "Stress Management: How Resilient Are You?" at **http://www.webmd.com/balance/stress-management/resilience-quiz.**

CHAPTER 3
1. You can read more about Anna Halprin and her work in my first book, *Women Dreaming-into-Art: Seven Artists Who Create from Dreams,* available on my website **www.TransitionTherapist.com** or on **www.galdepress.com.**

CHAPTER 4 2. If you are interested in finding out more about dreams and dreaming, read my book, *Bridging Night and Day: Decoding the Hidden Messages of Your Dreams.* You can order this book by going on my website: www.TransitionTherapist.com or through the publisher: **www.phoenixpublshinggroup.net**
3. Source: Adler, M. G., & Fagley, N. S. (2005). "Appreciation: Individual Differences in Finding Value and Meaning as a Unique Predictor of Subjective Well-Being." *Journal of Personality,* 73 (1), 79-114.

CHAPTER 6
4. Black swan theory was developed by Nassim Nicholas Taleb, who writes about how unexpected and rare events, or black swans, can have considerable impact in creating change.
5. For more information, go to:
http://citiscope.org/story/2014/comparing-mdgs-and-sdgs#sthash.Jup27apM.dpuf
6. This is a modified version of an exercise from *How to Master Change in Your Life: Sixty-Seven Ways to Handle Life's Toughest Moments* by Mary Carrol Moore. Minneapolis, MN: ECKANKAR, 1997.

Navigating Change: How to Go from Trauma to Transformation

BIBLIOGRAPHY

Ariadne, Patricia. *Drinking the Dragon: Stories of the Dark Night of Soul.* San Diego: Sirius Publications, 2009.

Ariadne, Patricia. *Drinking the Dragon: Stories of the Dark Night of Soul Process Workbook.* San Diego: Sirius Publications, 2010.

Bly, Robert. *The Sibling Society.* New York, New York: Addison-Wesley Publishing Co., 1996.

Bridges, William. *Transitions: Making Sense of Life's Changes.* Cambridge, MA: Perseus Books Group, 2004.

Chodron, Pema. *Living Beautifully with Uncertainty and Change.* Boston: MA: Shambhala, 2012. When Things Fall Apart: Heart Advice for Difficult Times. Boston, MA: Shambhala, 2000.

Dyer, Wayne. *Excuses Begone!: How to Change Lifelong, Self-Defeating Thinking Habits.* Carlsbad, CA: Hay House Publications, 2010.

Gladwell, Malcolm. *Outliers: The Story of Success.* New York, New York: Little, Brown and Co., 2008.

Huber, Cheri. *Making a Change for Good: A Guide to Compassionate Self-Discipline.* Boston, MA: Shambhala, 2007.

Moore, Mary Carrol. *How to Master Change in Your Life: Sixty-Seven Ways to Handle Life's Toughest Moments.* Minneapolis, MN: ECKANKAR, 1997.

Phipps, Carter. *Evolutionaries: Unlocking the Spiritual and Cultural Potential of Science's Greatest Idea.* New York, New York: HarperCollins, 2012.

Siebert, Al. *The Survivor Personality: Why Some People Are Stronger, Smarter, and More Skillful at Handling Life's Difficulties...and How You Can Be, Too.* New York, New York: The Berkley Publishing Group, 1996.

Strauss, William and Neil Howe. *The Fourth Turning: An American Prophecy.* New York, New York: Bantam Doubleday Dell Publishing Group, 1997.

Taleb, Nassim Nicholas. *Antifragile: Things That Gain from Disorder.* New York, New York: Random House, 2012.

Navigating Change: How to Go from Trauma to Transformation

APPENDICES

LIFE EVENTS STRESS SCALE

(The Social Readjustment Rating Scale)

To learn the level of stress-distress in your life, mark down the points for each event that you have experienced in the last 12 months. Depending on your coping skills, this scale can predict the likelihood that you may contract a stress-related illness. (The Social Readjustment Rating Scale was created by Thomas Rholmes and Richard Rahe, University of Washington School of Medicine).

0-149 = Low susceptibility to stress-related illness (30% chance or more)
150-299 = Medium susceptibility to stress-related illness (50% chance or more)
300+ = High susceptibility to stress-related illness (80% chance or more)

When you have finished checking the events below, add up the points for each event. Add your score to the bottom line.

	Points	Event
_____	100	Death of a spouse
_____	73	Divorce
_____	65	Marital or relationship partner separation
_____	63	Jail term
_____	63	Death of close family member
_____	53	Personal injury or illness
_____	50	Marriage
_____	47	Fired from work
_____	45	Marital reconciliation
_____	44	Change in family member's health
_____	40	Pregnancy
_____	39	Sex difficulties
_____	39	Addition to family
_____	39	Business readjustment
_____	38	Change in financial status
_____	37	Death of close friend
_____	36	Change to a different line of work
_____	35	Change in number of marital arguments
_____	31	Mortgage or loan over $150,000
_____	30	Foreclosure of mortgage or loan
_____	29	Change in work responsibilities
_____	29	Trouble with in-laws
_____	28	Outstanding personal achievement
_____	26	Spouse begins or stops work
_____	26	Starting or finishing schools
_____	25	Change in living conditions

_____	24	Revision of personal habits
_____	23	Trouble with boss
_____	20	Change in work hours, conditions
_____	20	Change in residence
_____	20	Change in schools
_____	19	Change in recreational habits
_____	19	Change in church activities
_____	18	Change in social activities
_____	17	Mortgage or loan under $150,000
_____	16	Change in sleeping habits
_____	15	Change in number of family gatherings
_____	15	Change in eating habits
_____	13	Vacation
_____	12	Christmas season
_____	11	Minor violations of the law

_____ YOUR TOTAL SCORE

DARK NIGHT OF SOUL PROCESS WORKBOOK

Dark Night of Soul Self-Test Inventory

Not At All	Somewhat	Average	Most of The Time	All of The Time
1	2	3	4	5

1. Recently, I have been feeling that life is passing me by. _____
2. I have a yearning for more meaning in my life. _____
3. Everything seems to have come to a dead-end. _____
4. I cannot seem to cope with day-to-day challenges. _____
5. I have experienced a crisis that has changed my life. _____
6. My dreams have been wilder in recent months. _____
7. I am disappointed with my accomplishments in life. _____
8. I feel like a failure. _____
9. I do not feel understood by family or friends. _____
10. I feel God has forsaken me. _____
11. I fear aging and physical decline. _____
12. I am afraid of death. _____
13. I am beginning to think about my legacy. _____
14. There are days when I can barely get out of bed. _____
15. My eating habits have changed. _____
16. My sleeping patterns have changed. _____
17. I am dissatisfied with my job. _____
18. My former life was too concerned with superficial things. _____
19. I am awkward or inept in communicating these days. _____
20. I have lost some of the things I depended upon in life. _____
21. Family, friends don't understand what is happening to me. _____
22. I am experiencing grief, sadness, regret. _____
23. I think I have wasted much of my life. _____
24. I wonder if there is a divine plan to life or if all is random. _____
25. I am more withdrawn from outside activities. _____
26. I have far less energy than before. _____
27. I have odd bodily symptoms, e.g. twitches, tingling, rash. _____
28. I am considering praying or meditating. _____
29. I may need to see a psychotherapist or spiritual advisor. _____

30. I worry what others are thinking or saying about me. _____
31. With recent losses, I am not sure of who I am. _____
32. I feel bereft, empty. _____
33. Childhood wounds and conflicts seem to be surfacing. _____
34. I am thinking of harming myself or ending it all. _____
35. I feel I have no support from family or friends. _____
36. I think that I am going through a mere "bump" in life. _____
37. I want a personal relationship with God or Life Force. _____

Explanation of Scoring:

To score, add up the number value for each answer: 5+4+1+3 and so on, until you have a total score. Then check the following page for the interpretation of this number.

If you scored between **226-250**, you may need to see a medical doctor or psychiatrist for a medical and mental health evaluation. If your anxiety and depression or other symptoms become so severe that you are not able to function or cannot reflect on your situation in life, you may need to check whether you require medication or some other type of professional support. If your thoughts lean toward suicide or self-harm, or you are not able to care for yourself, it may be that you will need hospitalization or inpatient care in a facility oriented toward spiritual emergencies. You should call a local crisis line or 911 if you do not know of a specific psychiatrist or other medical professional to contact.

If you scored **200-225**, you are in the place where you definitely need to find allies—some kind of regular spiritual counseling, support, or care; a general physical check-up by allopathic and homeopathic doctors ; and the guidance of spiritual scriptures and books. It would be helpful if you could take vacation time or sick leave to rest and to spend quiet time with reduced or absent TV, computer, and telephone use. Take this time to work with your dreams, to journal, to work in the *Dark Night of the Soul Process Workbook* (see the Bibliography at the back of this book) to rest and to take long walks, to pray or meditate, to work in a garden or to cook nurturing soups.

If you scored **150-199**, you would benefit from sessions with a spiritually-oriented psychotherapist or practitioner. Work in the *Dark Night of Soul Process Workbook* as well as with other self-help tools. It would be helpful for you to study your dreams, to journal, and to seek more time alone in order to reassess and reevaluate your life goals and spiritual progress. Read poetry, take walks in nature, draw or paint, pray or meditate.

If you scored **149** and below, you may be going through an emotional "slump" or challenge, but you will likely pull out of it in a natural progression of time. Talking with friends or a trusted older confidante, writing in your journal, and getting a lot of rest, eating well, and exercising would be helpful to your healing.

DISCLAIMER:

This inventory is for information purposes only. It is not a medical or psychological test and is not meant to take the place of professional evaluation or assessment by a licensed professional.

(Self-Test from *The Dark Night of Soul Process Workbook* by Dr. Patricia Ariadne, Ph.D. at **www.TransitionTherapist.com**)

THE FOUR R'S FOR REDUCING STRESS

RETREAT - When conflict becomes overwhelming:
- walk away
- try to take a time-out or period of reflection
- imagine humorous or realistic solutions

REFRAME - View crises as creative choices; you can choose how to respond! A few recommendations:
- use a soft voice, an open mind, suggest new ideas/solutions
- instead of looking at things personally, try to view things objectively
- remember successes, victories, reasons for hope

RELATE - balance stress and conflict with:
- exercise
- fun- go to the beach, see a movie
- family and friends

REACH OUT - Think "we" instead of "me":
- do an anonymous kindness for another
- volunteer at a senior center or school
- call, write or email someone to thank them

Dr. Ariadne's Books

Women Dreaming-into-Art: Seven Women Who Create from Dreams. Lakeville, MN: Galde Press, 2006. (Buy on Amazon or TransitionTherapist.com).

Drinking the Dragon: Stories of the Dark Night of Soul, Second Edition. San Diego, CA: Sothis Press, 2016. (Buy on Amazon or at TransitionTherapist.com)

Drinking the Dragon: Process Workbook, Second Edition. San Diego, CA: Sothis Press, 2016 (Buy on Amazon or at TransitionTherapist.com).

Marjorie Klemp: Her Spiritual Journey through Service. Kindle eBook, September, 2012. (Buy on Amazon)

Transition Series:
Bridging Night & Day: Decoding the Hidden Messages of Your Dreams. Sothis Press, 2016. (Buy online at Amazon or TransitionTherapist.com)

Navigating Change: How to Go from Trauma to Transformation. Sothis Press, 2016. (Buy on Amazon or TransitionTherapist.com)

Made in United States
Troutdale, OR
07/02/2023

10945805R00064